O9-BHK-808

The Structure of Awareness

UNIVERSITY OF ILLINOIS PRESS
Urbana Chicago London

THE STRUCTURE
OF AWARENESS

Introduction to a Situational
Theory of Truth and Knowledge

D. W. GOTSHALK

ONCE MORE
TO
NAOMI

Preface

Knowledge has always been a problem for philosophers. This may seem peculiar. Everyone knows what knowledge is. Why not philosophers? However, when a person is asked to state his views, to describe in coherent pattern the empirical and a priori, meaning and syntax, and all the other recognized or alleged components of knowledge, he soon discovers that what philosophers have puzzled over for many years is still a considerable puzzle.

This book is an effort to put the pieces of this puzzle together in a distinctive way. I have called it an introduction to a situational theory of truth and knowledge. It concentrates at the outset on the aim-structure of awareness as the organizing principle of the knowledge situation and of the domain of knowledge. In this way it approaches the questions of what knowledge is and what knowledge does, which seem to us the primary philosophical problems of knowledge. To some, a more urgent and formidable problem is the future of knowledge. At present, knowledge, especially in the physical, chemical, and biological sciences, is expanding at an enormous rate, arousing mixed emotions. Where are we heading? The demonic and apocalyptic mingle with the euphoric and utopian in forecasts of the future of knowledge. The answer to this problem, I think, depends to some extent on factors outside knowledge. But it also depends rather decisively, I shall contend, on the way these outside factors affect the aim-structure of cognitive consciousness.

The main thesis of this book may be stated very briefly. The aim in knowledge is awareness, awareness of what is the case; and truth is any symbolic array, a written report for example, that provides the awareness required in a situation by this cognitive aim. By "situation" I mean any configuration of items forming the field of cognitive attention. "Modern situation," "world situation," and "knowledge situation" illustrate the term as well as an immediate personal condition. Truth is not pie-in-the-sky, a floating abstraction. It is concrete, "working," functional, and any symbolic array meeting the demands of awareness in a situation is true, a truth, or the truth, even if it is local, trivial, incomplete in certain abstract ways, or otherwise lacking in traditional perfections.

The argument of this book begins with a brief depiction of the broad domain of knowledge. Two chapters follow in which the characteristic cognitive activities of observation and theory construction are considered. In the four succeeding chapters, the major components of knowledge, its materials, form, content, and functions are analyzed. The book concludes with a statement of what our social situation seems to require of the domain of knowledge today. The argument pretends to give no exhaustive account of its topics. Some of them would require a book for that. Its aim is simply to introduce the structural or situational approach by such discussion of the elements of knowledge as seems sufficient to do this.

I wish to record my gratitude to the many writers on theory of knowledge past and present, particularly those cited in the text and notes. Their work has been invaluable to me in many respects, and not least as a challenge to attempt to formulate a theory of knowledge that gives prominence to the structure of awareness and the situational approach.

D. W. G.

Contents

I

Knowledge as a Domain

The Aim

A domain, as I shall interpret it, is any area of human activity having an established and distinctive purpose structure. Transportation, law, journalism, and politics are among countless illustrations of domains. Each includes many human activities along fairly well-established lines, and each has a purpose—a different purpose. Law is not transportation, nor does it aim to be. Similarly, journalism, politics, and the others are distinct despite many connections and common attributes. Domains often exist inside domains or as subdomains. A culture may be defined as a system of domains located at a certain time and place with their subdomains included.[1]

Unquestionably the leading element of a domain is its aim or purpose structure. This differentiates a domain since it indicates the characteristic direction of its activities. The aims of a lawyer are many, as are those of a transport worker. But a lawyer handling a case in court is not moving cargo from place to place. Nor is a journalist at his desk, nor a politician considering his next move. In their charac-

[1] Cf. D. W. Gotshalk, *Patterns of Good and Evil* (Urbana: University of Illinois Press, 1963), chap. 6.

1

teristic jobs, agents such as these have very different aims, and these aims differentiate their activities. Thus, the first step in interpreting a domain as individuated or set off from other domains would seem to be to discover its differentiating aim.

In regard to knowledge, I suggest, the characteristic aim of its activities is awareness of what is the case, and any activity in any situation is cognitive to the extent that it possesses this aim. This aim may be combined with many others: to win a lawsuit, to transport cargo, to write a good piece of journalism, etc. But no one of these other aims is necessary to distinguish an end-directed activity as cognitive. On the other hand, when the aim or goal of an activity is awareness of a situation or of items in that situation, the activity is cognitive and belongs to the domain of knowledge.

Activity guided by this aim may take numerous specific directions. There are many subdomains of knowledge. It may be addressed to the most diverse entities from a minor detail to the total universe. Copernicus writes:

I found at length by much and long observation, that if the motions of the other planets were added to the rotation of the earth, and calculated as for the revolution of that planet, not only the phenomena of the others followed from this, but that it so bound together both the order and magnitudes of all the planets and the spheres and the heaven itself that in no single part could one thing be altered without confusion among the other parts and in all the Universe. Hence for this reason . . . I have followed this system.[2]

This Copernican awareness of the unity of the universe on the basis of his "system" is a peak achievement of the cognitive aim. But it is typical of the kind of achievement sought in any field where the aim is to face a situation and win knowledge of it.

[2] Quoted in E. A. Burtt, *Metaphysical Foundations of Modern Science* (New York: Harcourt, Brace & Co., 1925), p. 37.

Awareness as an aim has a directional or vector structure. There is movement toward a goal, which springs from impulse directed toward an outcome. This goalward impulse of awareness as an aim is original in several respects. It is not implanted from without. Neither society nor physical existence need instruct us for the impulse to be there. Indeed, they could not instruct us unless the impulse were already there, since instruction means giving the impulse specific direction, leading it to a particular item or array of items. The impulse is original in another sense. It does not derive its characteristic being from more primitive impulses. Hunger, sex, and the other impulses may use it and sharpen it. But they are not competent to endow it with its unique nature. In function and goal the aim is separate and distinct. Its goal is enlightenment, not sexual satisfaction or reprieve from hunger. It is *sui generis* in this respect, as any other elementary constituent of our being.

Awareness as an aim may also be described as the organizing principle of the domain of knowledge. Its directional or vector structure enters into all of the domain's components. It shapes the processes of observation and theory construction. It uses the materials, forms, contents, and functions of the product of these processes for its own purposes. It also furnishes the primary standard of value for measuring items as knowledge. I should say at once that cognition will be interpreted throughout our discussions as a value activity. Indeed, I believe there is no escaping values in any human activity.[3] In the domain of knowledge the distinctive standard of value is the aim that directs its processes and makes certain demands of its products. Within its own realm, where it is not subservient to other ends, this aim with its requirements determines what is valuable as knowledge and as contributing to knowledge in each individual case. Accordingly, the aim with its di-

[3] Gotshalk, *Patterns of Good and Evil*, chap. 6.

rectional structure enters determinately into all the elements of the domain of knowledge: observation, theory construction, symbol selection, and value attainment, and gives them their characteristic shape and thrust. This is what is meant by describing it as the organizing principle of the domain.

Knowledge is always knowledge *of:* knowledge of persons, places, things, even knowledge of knowledge. What more precisely is its field?

The Field

The intellectual life, the knowledge-seeking and knowledge-enjoying life, and the domain of knowledge itself include activities of great diversity. The artist who discusses ideas about his craft or about another artist's work, the politician who expounds in public forum his theory of legislation, the industrialist who has worked out his views of the proper relations between labor and management, are operating in the intellectual domain as definitely as the scientist studying the nature of particles or the philosopher seeking an adequate conception of the universe. They may not know it. They may not want to. But only where knowledge is used with overwhelming concern for transcognitive purposes is the intellectual life truly submerged: a practiced cook making a mince pie, a skilled driver steering his auto through heavy traffic. In such cases, major attention is given to cooking and steering, not to knowledge. Knowledge is present, often plentifully, but its assertion is not the focal concern of the agent or activity.

Even so, the extent of the domain of knowledge remains enormous. Wherever a cognitive claim is made, wherever an activity consists of devising, entertaining, or expounding an account of things that claims to be accurate, the intellectual life comes into focus. The account may be utterly wrong. Things may be entirely different.

But the claim is the telltale mark, indicating the aim, and sets off the intellectual endeavor from all others. I say "an account of things that claims to be accurate." This may include the claim of a cook that his recipe for mince pie will produce a certain kind of pie, or the claim of an auto driver that his views of traffic control will prevent certain types of auto accidents. These are expounded statements, not transcognitive actions. They are claimed to be knowledge. Especially notable here are value statements: the claim of a veterinarian that a certain kind of treatment is harmful to a dog's health, the claim of an enthusiast that life in a certain locale is the ideal life for a human being or for a certain type of human being. When these statements are set forth as accurate accounts, they are as much grist for the intellectual mill as the generalizations of a physicist or the formulae of an astronomer. The important point is not what claims or statements are about, but what they purport to claim. Where they claim to be correct reports, such statements, true or false, become intellectual challenges. They invite cognitive scrutiny, and invoke the critical operations of the domain of knowledge.

Since statements making a cognitive claim have really no topical limit, the intellectual life and the domain of knowledge might be said to extend to anything and everything. This inclusive terrain is commonly called the world or universe, and the characteristic business of knowledge and knowing might be said to be to sharpen our awareness of the nature of our world, or of the situations and features of the things in our universe. For present purposes no detailed picture of this territory is necessary. Our topic is theory of knowledge, not theory of the universe. Generally, I shall assume the commonsense view. I shall assume a world exhibiting a spread of things in space and time, and a flow of events in causal sequences with achieved termini or outcomes. The precise philosophical meaning

6 The Structure of Awareness

of some of these terms—"things," "events," "space," "time," "causal," "termini"—is provided elsewhere.[4] Unless otherwise indicated, I shall keep to their meanings in ordinary discourse.

In addition, I shall assume one other feature of the universe, included in the commonsense view, and calling for special comment: The universe includes people no less than things and events, and people as knowers. This statement may seem gratuitous. But when some philosophers think of knowledge, they think of science, and when they think of science, they think of natural or physical science, the knowledge of physical things. But people are in the world we know as totally as are stars and molecules, and I mean here people, not as physical things, as colloidal solutions or molecular clusters, but as persons with hopes and aims and dreams and disappointments. Our modern world has turned the great lens of exact knowledge in one direction, exploring deeply the intricacies of natural things in their mechanical connections. But the domains of goal-directed human activities, including natural science itself which is a goal-directed activity, are just as much there to be studied and known as any physical process, and in some ways they are more urgent and promising objects of knowledge, as we shall see.

The traditional philosophical view that places the *cognitive* subject outside the field of knowledge should not be understood as accepted in our account. Customarily, it is said, the knowledge situation consists of a subject and an object. The subject knows. The object is what is known. The object stands over against the subject, and thus the subject stands outside what is known. This analysis may apply to certain situations, such as a casual glance at external things. But even in a good deal of ordinary know-

[4] D. W. Gotshalk, *Structure and Reality* (New York: Dial Press, 1937; New York: Greenwood Press, 1968).

ing of externals we are aware that we are knowing. The knower as knowing, no less than his external object, is in the orbit of his awareness. Indeed, this self-consciousness is one of the unique features of human experience. The animal may know objects, but, as Leibniz remarked, it is doubtful that he knows he is an animal. The paradox of the traditional position is that the problem of knowledge could not arise, and would not be soluble, if the human being did not know that he was a knower and that knowing was an activity of his. And when I say the human being knows he is a knower, I mean that he knows himself as subject and as he functions as subject, not as a traditionally conceived object. It is of the essence of knowledge to understand what it is to be an active knower, a live subject.

A Priori

The universe as the field of cognition, then, consists of a large multiplicity of entities existing in space, time, and other ontological orders such as causality. The common-sense view is that in cognition these entities and orders are discovered and not made by the knower, except, of course, where the knower physically alters what he is studying as he might in a laboratory experiment. A traditional view, however, divides the field of cognition into two halves: the a priori and the empirical. The entities and their contents are discovered and empirical. The pervading orders are made by the knowing mind, and a priori. Kant, who held such a view, described the a priori orders as created in a dark chamber of the soul. Unsurprisingly, no one has ever witnessed this occurrence, nor the injection by the knowing mind of the universal spatial, temporal, or other ontological orders of our world into the natural entities of existence. The view remains a pure speculation. Kant had, however, another and distinct meaning of a priori. The a priori is the universal and necessary. I believe this can be made into a serviceable conception, but to do so a distinction must be drawn that Kant did not draw. This is between the universal and necessary *for* knowledge and the universal and necessary *in* knowledge.

By the universal and necessary *for* knowledge is meant whatever is universally required besides the knowing process for the knowledge we have to occur. In this sense, the universe and its pervading patterns of space, time, etc. would be a priori since all of these seem necessary for our having the kind of everyday and scientific knowledge we have. However, Kant's manifold of sensibility, the empirical data fed into the knowing process by things-in-themselves, would also be a priori in this sense, since this manifold is everywhere required for our everyday and scientific knowledge of objects, according to Kant. On this usage of a priori, therefore, the distinction between the a priori and the empirical would become considerably blurred in following Kant.

In contrast, the a priori *in* knowledge refers to a constituent of the inner structure of knowledge. This constituent is invariant and universal as distinguished from variable and contingent. The obvious illustration of this a priori is the general knowledge aim. I prefer however to limit the term to the requirements or necessities everywhere imposed on knowledge by this aim. These necessities I believe are of two sorts, and these shall constitute the primary meaning of a priori in our account of knowledge.

The first of these requirements or necessities *in* knowledge is formal. It is epitomized by the laws of logic. To be knowledge, a cognition must be coherent or consistent. Incoherent or contradictory, it tells us nothing about an item that it does not also blur or deny, and so thwarts or negates the aim of awareness. The general laws of logic, such as identity and contradiction, embody the formal principles of coherence and consistency, and as universal structural requirements, they epitomize the formal type of a priori *in* knowledge.

The second sort of a priori springing from the cognitive aim concerns the materials of knowledge. It is a principle of specific material selection. By materials I shall mean that of which knowledge is composed. Just as a house is made of stone or a table of wood, so knowledge is made of something. This something I shall call "symbols," and I shall describe knowing as a symbolizing process and knowledge as a structure of symbols. (I shall discuss symbols more fully later.) In dealing with the universe, the cognitive activity explores a great variety of items. To record accurately and specifically the diverse items of this great variety some principle of symbolic selection beyond consistency seems needed. After all, our concepts of "iron," "gravitation," and "labor leader" may all be coherent and consistent. But to be useful they also must be different since they symbolize different things. Some principle of symbolic selection that recognizes these differences therefore must function in the formation of these concepts.

It may be thought that "the facts themselves" could serve as such a principle. They could sift out the irrelevant and the fanciful, and specifically unfold what a concept or other symbolic structure as knowledge should contain. Such object control by facts does describe crudely an important feature of certain knowledge transactions. For example, where the knower is analyzing an observable set of entities, he is customarily guided by his awareness of these entities, and in this indirect sense the object may be said to be controlling his symbolic formations. But actually it is the awareness of the knower with its vectorial structure that is in control and shaping his symbolic formations to comply with the requirements of the cognitive aim.

The second major a priori *in* knowledge might be

described as the principle of material necessity. It is a principle demanding that any concept or symbolic structure admitted as knowledge in any situation must be able to provide, or contribute to providing, the object-awareness required by the cognitive aim in that situation. If a symbol, such as "phlogiston" or "demons," does not do this, it is cognitively inadmissible, no matter how important it may be from a practical, religious, or other transcognitive standpoint. On the other hand, if such a symbol is genuinely or probably required for this purpose, it must be admitted as a genuine or probable component of the concept or other symbolic account of the field or item. There must be a sufficient reason for any symbol being a constituent of a concept or other symbolic structure admitted as knowledge, and material necessity is the principle of sufficient reason *in* knowledge.

In this discussion, I have been suggesting a certain conception of a concept: as a normative structure of symbols governed by a selective principle. I shall return to this conception in subsequent chapters. Meanwhile, in summary of some main thoughts in this section and the preceding sections of this chapter, let me describe the knowledge enterprise as facing two ways. It faces toward a universe of diversified being in which everything can be found, and it faces toward a goal of its own. Also it seeks to realize its goal in its own medium of symbols, placing certain a priori or universal and necessary restrictions on these symbols. The symbolic arrays that compose knowledge are required to be well-formed forms, coherent and consistent, independent of the items or field being investigated. They are also required to include those symbols and all of those symbols, no more but no less, that are necessary for the fulfillment in the specific differentiated situation of the cognitive aim.

While certain universal principles of knowledge may

be a priori, the variety of content of knowledge is commonly believed to be "empirical" or derived from experience, and empirical is commonly contrasted with the a priori as a constituent of knowledge. What does "empirical" mean in this connection? What does "experience" mean?

Empirical

The term "symbol" as describing the material of knowledge must be understood in a very broad sense. It must not be limited to certain standardized entities such as words or mathematical terms, and certainly not to "poetic" symbols, for example, whiteness as a symbol of purity. The point may be put in this way. Awareness itself, including averbal and preverbal awareness, is symbolizing, or an instance of symbolic functioning. It is the recording in one's being of whatever is the end-point of attention. This end-point may be the pleasure-pain condition of one's body, or it may be environing states and things. But, whatever it is, whenever there is awareness of it, there is symbolizing, and whatever is used for this symbolizing—sensations, feelings, images, or any other alingual or prelingual psychological material, no less than words—are symbols in our sense.

Presumably, if awareness is symbolizing and experience is our first form of awareness, symbolizing starts with experience, and all of our original symbols are empirical. There are no innate ideas in the sense of pre-empirical symbols. Language and other symbolic systems were first invented to articulate, communicate, and extend awareness. Now they are taught to initiate the unlearned into established public articulations or institutionalized forms of our awareness. As awareness increases, broadens, or becomes more refined, new terms and new uses of old terms are added, and language and similar symbolic systems grow. This growth commonly springs from a movement of mind recording new actualities and possibilities in action and existence rather than from a mere mechanical accumulation of external items.

Sometimes those who hold the empiricist view of the origin of ideas, such as positivists, following distantly John Locke and David Hume, limit experiencing to sensing, or, in our terms, to the recording in the knower of the sense-qualities of external things and the introspective features of psychological states. But if experience is symbolizing, and if in our experiential commerce with the items of the world we record their imaginative suggestions, their adequacy to our needs, and more, then experience— and I mean cognitive experience—cannot be limited merely to sensing or to the boundaries of traditional Empiricism. Just what range should be assigned to experience will be discussed in the next chapter.

Symbols as material compose knowledge as a product, and knowledge as a product might be described in a preliminary way as the outcome of a collaboration of empirical material with a priori requirements. The intellectual life however is commonly thought of as a process rather than a product, and a process ordinarily occurring in a setting of activities constituting the culture or civilization of an age. Some general characterization of the processes of cognition and their cultural setting should therefore be given to complete this preliminary account of knowledge as a domain.

Activity

The domain of knowledge as all others is an area of activity. Sometimes this activity itself is called knowledge. This position is taken not merely by instrumentalists, operationalists, pragmatists, and similar philosophers. "My knowledge is activity," Stravinsky says. "I discover it as I work, and I know it while I am discovering it, but only in a very different way before and after." [5] This view may seem to confuse "knowledge" and "know-how." In any case, in our discussions I shall follow more conventional usage, describing the activity of the knowledge domain as knowing and its distinctive end-product only as knowledge. Throughout, however, I shall interpret knowledge as basically functional, a result produced for an end and having value as working for this end, and everywhere I shall interpret the *domain* of knowledge itself as primarily an area of activity.

This activity is the topic of the next two chapters, but a general characterization of it may be helpful at this point. First, it is a creative activity. Knowledge is not innate, ready-made in the mind, at least not the knowledge we have and know. Nor is it acquired by passively allowing an influx of sensations. Knowledge is constructed. It is the handiwork of awareness operating in its own behalf. Knowing is as original and natural with the human being as breathing or screaming. It begins with human life itself, with the first awakenings, and the intellectual life prosperously developed is merely a sustained spreading effort to improve this condition and to attain a heightened awakening.

Knowing, I say, is creative. It is giving birth to the original and new. Starting with initial awareness, it is a recording of inner or outer items of the world in a consciousness. This recording is a refabrication of the world in symbols, a brand-new addition. It is an attainment in a new medium following an original inner direction. Only secondarily and superficially is knowledge ever a handout of preformed material from social sources. Its roots are deep inside the human person, enshrined in an original endowment, and except in its most derivative form, it does not ever lose the tang and flavor of the individual human

[5] Igor Stravinsky and Robert Craft, *Memories and Commentaries* (Garden City, N.Y.: Doubleday & Co., 1960), p. 108.

knower. These remarks are not meant to disparage the role of the social context in the knowledge process. The civilization in which the knower exists and flourishes usually has an enormous influence upon him. But, however this may be, knowledge begins with the knower, with his transforming act of symbolization—creating a world within a world. All the social influence in the universe would be of no avail in knowledge without this creative capacity of the knower.

The knowledge domain, despite the extensive field I have assigned to it, is not all-comprehensive. Human living is more than knowing, and even the intellectual seeks from his existence more than the heightened awareness provided by knowing. Yet the domain of knowledge is also not a segregated and merely specialized area. It extends into all four corners of human life. The intellectual will use knowledge in his ordinary everyday actions, sometimes skillfully, sometimes badly, and he will do all manner of things in accordance with his awareness of situations. But so will any other human being. It is for this reason that a culture or civilization, the cluster of large-scale domain activities existing together at a certain time and place, penetrates into the knowledge domain. It makes all sorts of demands on knowledge because its various areas, war and politics, travel and poetry, and many more, are regions of activity involving awareness. Knowledge is everywhere integral to what a civilization is doing, and the demands of a civilization, therefore, will inevitably reach into its innermost precincts, and shape its development sometimes in a very complicated manner.

These brief remarks on the integrality of civilization and knowledge will be amplified in Chapter VIII. But much more should be said at once about the activities of the knowledge domain which carry out its structural aim and impart to it its fundamentally dynamic character. The first of these activities is observation.

II

Observation

General Nature

Observation is both knowing and a method of knowing. In its general nature, therefore, we should come close to the central character of all cognition. As commonly understood, observation is sense-monitored cognition directed to things in the surrounding environment. I observe the clouds in the sky, the automobiles in the street, my neighbor tipping his hat to a passing lady. I also notice that my head aches, my joints burn, and I am not feeling well. Is this noticing also observation?

The range of observation will be our topic in a moment. Let us look further into its nature. Observation is knowing, which means that it is symbolizing, a recording in the being of the knower of the items that the knower is said to be observing. Ordinarily, in the mature adult, the terms in which he expresses his observations are words or other standardized symbols. But these are not necessarily or even usually the terms in which his observations occur. These terms are more usually sensations of various types, odors and pressures and sights and sounds, also fleeting suggestions, including some of those extraordinary nuances that require a Proust for explicit description. The marvelous

16   *The Structure of Awareness*

silent recording of objects in these psychological terms, illumined by our background, goes on all during the time we look and touch and listen with any attention, and the vast arsenal of standardized symbols—verbal, musical, mathematical, etc.—usually explicates only a fraction of the knowledge we create and store during these acts of attention.

But *is* this knowledge? Certainly in some sense it is. Sometimes observation is described as passive, a mere receiving of raw materials that need the work of the mind to be converted into knowledge. But even the most elementary desultory observation is more than this. First, the "raw" materials of knowledge do not come from the observed universe. The world gives off no epistemological effluvia. In the epistemological transaction, unless it is altered by other agencies than the knower's awareness, the area of the universe under observation remains what it is. In this transaction, only the awareness of the knower is added. Second, this awareness of the knower is an activity. It is passive only in the sense that it does not alter physically the clouds and automobiles and other entities of which it is aware: it is merely aware of them. But this awareness itself is an active translation of observed items into records, sensations, images, feeling tones, etc., and these records as portraying what is the case are knowledge. In many instances this knowledge may be "raw" or "crude" in the sense of trivial or transient or no longer needed, or in the more usual sense of requiring certain refinements to enter usefully into more developed structures, such as standard vocabulary expressions, plans for practical action, theories in science or philosophy. But if one were able to observe in the manner of such observation every last detail in the entire universe—past, present, future, actual and possible, physical and psychological—and hold all of them in one grand coherent self-conscious act of awareness, one would really possess all knowledge, and have attained all that standard vocabulary expressions, practical plans, science, and philosophy can attain in cognitive achievement. Of course human observation as we know it is far more limited. Not only does a great deal of it provide only a kind of raw or crude knowledge in the senses already mentioned, but even with the assistance of physical instruments it leaves continents of entities unengaged. The vast regions of the subperceptual and the superperceptual, open to theory construction, are not open to that face-to-face confrontation in human perception that is part of the general meaning of observation.

Scope

What is the scope of observation? I have said that I observe clouds and automobiles and my neighbor. But some philosophers would say that I observe none of these. For example, I think I observe an automobile, but, according to these philosophers, what I observe are colors, lines, and shapes, which I "interpret" or think of as an "automobile." I observe sensa or sense-data, but not things or people which are really inferred from sense-data.

This sense-data theory, which originated in modern times during the era of Descartes and Locke, was in vogue in the first half of this century. But recently it has come under criticism from many quarters. We shall consider a few of these criticisms later on.[1] But here, as a theory of observation, the theory has the fatal defect of not describing what ordinarily we do observe. We do observe automobiles, and, generally, persons, places, and things, and in driving along a highway sometimes we scarcely

[1] See Friedrich Waismann, "Verifiability," *Logic and Language*, ed. A. Flew, first series (Oxford: Blackwell & Co., 1951), pp. 117-44; A. J. Ayer, *The Problem of Knowledge* (Baltimore: Penguin Books, 1956), pp. 118-29; N. R. Hanson, *Patterns of Discovery* (Cambridge: Cambridge University Press, 1961), pp. 7, 21, 22.

notice the color, line, or texture of a car, so keen are we
to take it in as an individual moving thing. Moreover, we
observe it as an individual or unit directly, without con-
scious inference. In the great majority of ordinary cases
there is no "thinking" of what the thing is.[2] We know what
it is. Identifying concepts are integral functioning constitu-
ents of the act of observation, not added on. I say that this
is not the exceptional but the ordinary way of observing,
because ordinarily we have to deal with cars and persons
and the like as individuals, and we watch or try to watch
them in this way. It takes a very recondite and special
interest to limit ordinary direct observation to color, line,
or texture, an attitude of abstraction that is very remote
from the usual way of observing things.[3]

Such plausibility as the sense-data theory has had has
arisen in connection with error in the observation of objects. I say I observe my neighbor tipping his hat. But it
turns out that the person I was observing was a stranger,
not my neighbor. What I was actually observing, the
sense-data theorist tells me, were certain shapes and colors
and movement lines which I interpreted under the concept
"neighbor tipping hat." I did observe the data. The concept
"neighbor tipping hat" was an interpretation added to the
data and, as it turned out, a false interpretation although
the observational data were correct. This analysis, however, is open to an easy refutation. For in the present case,
at least I can properly say that I was not observing shapes
and colors and movement lines except incidentally. I was
observing an individual being. And it was this individual

[2] Charles A. Baylis, "Foundations for a Presentative Theory of Perception and Sensation," paper delivered at the Aristotelian Society
meeting, Jan. 31, 1966, p. 41 ff.
[3] Hanson, in *Patterns of Discovery,* p. 22, suggests that the purely
sense-datum response is characteristic of the infant and the idiot.
This seems a little unfair, unless Hanson includes in the latter such
people as painters and art connoisseurs, who sometimes concentrate
their observation on a color patch, a line, or texture.

being which I interpreted falsely and which I interpreted as my neighbor. It was not a multiplicity of shapes and colors and lines, which no one in his right mind would ordinarily interpret as his neighbor. Moreover, if it turned out that this being was not only not my neighbor but not a man—a gorilla say, or a machine, or anything you wish— the reply would be the same: I was observing an individual being but interpreting it falsely. The fact is that in ordinary situations we usually observe colors and lines and the like as properties of things. They are modifiers or adjectives, and customarily, unless we are particularly interested in these qualities, our attention in observation is directed to the individual things they modify which we may misidentify in various ways.

The misidentification of individual objects is of course only one type of error in observation. There are numerous others. But all of them can be equally explained, I believe, without resort to the sense-data theory. They arise from some fault in the observational apparatus or process.[4] A defect in a sense organ, tone-deafness or color-blindness, usually results in a defect in our observation of a sense quality. A similar consequence follows from a defect in our intuitive power, by which power I mean here our ability to perceive things and events in their spatial and temporal configurations as when we perceive a vase as a three-dimensional object or the ticking of a clock as a rhythmic sequence, a tick-tock sequence. Imagination, which is the power to apprehend the absent in the present, and specifically in observation the power to read the suggestions of an object about details not actually present, can easily go astray. One may imagine he is looking at a sharp knife because the edge of the knife has a bright gleam, and one may be as mistaken on this point as a person whose intuitive power led him to see all thin objects, such

[4] Baylis, "Foundations," p. 45 ff.

as knife blades, as flat or without spatial depth. A deranged feeling-state, a pathological horror of a certain type of situation, may result in our misobserving an innocuous object. Furthermore, observation in most mature human beings occurs within a sizable background of knowledge. "Observation of X is shaped by prior knowledge of X." [5] This knowledge integral to observation may be misapplied as in the misidentifications of objects already cited. Add to these sources of observational error in the knower the equally familiar distorting influences in the environment, particularly in physical media (e.g. blue-colored glasses, water in which a stick is immersed) and also the social pressures that may be exerted in the observational process (e.g. the use of advertisements to persuade people to see or taste or smell what is not the case), and the explanation of observational error by evident defects in the observational process seems perfectly competent to handle all the types of error usually cited, without recourse to any sense-data theory.

As against the sense-data theory, then, the range of observation includes persons and places and things [6] as well as sense-qualities and properties. Does it include psychological states? Some have suggested that the term "observation" be limited to observation of the physical, or to observation as it is in the physical sciences.[7] But this seems to be an unnecessary restriction. It also involves appreciable linguistic awkwardness. Strictly speaking, it means that many things that I notice, such as my psychological condition, I do not observe, and many things that I observe, I treat differently in principle from the things I

[5] Hanson, *Patterns of Discovery*, p. 19.
[6] See Roderick M. Chisholm, *Perceiving: A Philosophical Study* (Ithaca, N.Y.: Cornell University Press, 1957), p. 158; *idem, Theory of Knowledge* (Englewood Cliffs, N.J.: Prentice-Hall, 1966), p. 94 ff.
[7] John Yolton, *Thinking and Perceiving* (LaSalle, Ill.: Open Court Publishing Co., 1962).

notice. This seems contrary to common understanding and established usage. According to these, to notice a man swimming is to observe him briefly in some degree, and to notice a process in physical science and to observe it are not different in principle, only in intensity and extent. In what follows, therefore, I shall include psychological states, which we do notice, within the range of observation. But even with this addition, the range of observation remains markedly limited. It excludes innumerable entities of which human beings often seek knowledge, such as the middle-sized objects that populate or did populate the remote regions of space and time, and the very tiny and very large objects occupying the vast precincts of the subperceptual and the superperceptual. Moreover, some who would agree that psychological states are observable, would severely limit this possibility to observation of their own states. They might concede that we observe other people, and not merely sense-data about them. But we observe them only in an external way. What is psychologically inside them or in their minds is opaque to observation. In a sense, of course, this is obviously true. Certainly, I cannot observe the state of mind of my neighbor in the way he can in self-conscious awareness. However, my neighbor can observe his own state of mind there, and in this respect observation of psychological states is not limited to the examination of one's own "insides."

I think, however, we can go further than this. Consider the case of purpose and value. In important respects, these so-called inner factors are open to public observation. By definition, it is true, I cannot observe a purpose as an inner principle of another person, or a value as an inner satisfaction, if it is an inner satisfaction. But I can observe the actions of this person, and as I watch him shovel the snow off the sidewalk and stop and sigh and smile at the completion of this task, it seems evident from my observation that his actions were purpose-directed, and that clearing the sidewalk of snow had a value for him, although exactly what value I may not be sure I know. Human beings bring to the observation of others a wide knowledge of the patterns of human behavior and of their purposes and values, derived by various routes. From the external side they are able to identify many of these patterns and correlatives quite accurately, often far more accurately than they can identify subtle noises or recondite shades of color directly encountered. When they identify these, they are truly observing purpose in action, ends patterning behavior, and values in realization, in an external, yet genuine and substantial way. This conception of certain so-called inner factors such as purpose and value as having an external as well as an internal being is recognized in language as when we speak of a glance as "very determined," meaning "set purposefully on certain values." Indeed, many terms in our language besides value and purpose, "depression," "joy," and others, signify both a certain kind of behavior and a certain kind of inner state. The two are conceived as integral parts of the same whole. "Depressed" means feeling in a certain way and behaving in a certain manner. One aspect is as authentically signified by the term as the other.[8] Thus, there is no need to hold that what is meant by such a term as "feeling" or "purpose" or "value" is only an inner and private fact. In a definite sense, as exhibited in behavior, this fact is open to observational inspection and public scrutiny, and this has long been recognized in language.

Of course, competence in making such observations is not given to everyone in equal degree. A novelist may have it much more abundantly than others. Often it is a

[8] P. F. Strawson, *Individuals* (Garden City, N.Y.: Doubleday & Co., Anchor Books, 1963), p. 105. Behaviorism derives considerable plausibility from this circumstance, but commits the fallacy of taking the part for the whole.

function of talent. Yet even with ordinary people observation is not a mere mechanical and repetitive act. It is a living and growing process, and usually increases in range and depth as one's experience enlarges. The commonplace example of the neophyte and the veteran bacteriologist examining the same cell specimen under a microscope is the standard illustration of this phenomenon. Differences in quality of observation may be partly due to a person's native talent, his inborn agility. But in a marked degree it is also due to his background.

Background

Sensation, intuition, imagination, feeling, intellect or conceptual identification—the segments of observational awareness that I have already mentioned—might be described as a multipronged instrument operating in the foreground of the observational activity. They are really the awareness maintained in the knower by a unified neurocerebral apparatus that is extremely docile and capable of developing in consciousness an extraordinary symbolic record. This physiological counterpart in the knower, the neurocerebral apparatus, I shall largely take for granted. But it will always be presupposed, and I shall refer to it where such reference may be helpful.

If the segments of awareness mentioned above may be described as a kind of psychological machinery, in observation this machinery performs within a complex framework. Sometimes the framework protrudes. Usually it remains in the background. Generally two types of factors compose it.

There is the principle of direction of knowing activity, the goal for which an observation is undertaken. This goal may be pure knowledge, i.e., to become aware simply of what is the case in the situation being observed. In this endeavor the goal not only is the directional principle behind the observation, structuring its path, it also constitutes with its requirements a set of norms for judging the particular observational endeavor, determining the degree of success or failure of the observation as an effort after knowledge.

Even where the emphasis in observation is on pure awareness, other aims and standards may operate in the background. An observation directed to discover in the sharpest terms what is the case may be linked with testing a prediction or drawing an inference. Or it may be undertaken to better answer the question: How can I use this object?, where such a question has been followed by a *caveat:* "Let's first discover what the object is." Other purposes may lie in the background: to determine how the object may fit one's inclinations, its attractiveness or non-attractiveness on professional as well as personal grounds. All of these, and the demands put on an observation by the cognitive aim itself, compose a complex grading system for evaluating the knowledge quality of the observation and the stature of the observed object in various respects.

In the special sciences the observer often tries to abstract from all evaluation except of the knowledge as knowledge and its significance for theory. But we should not overlook the fact that this *is* evaluation, and that in this respect the special sciences are value enterprises. The introduction of extracognitive norms into the background of observation does not add an altogether new factor but merely enlarges a factor already present. "Even at the level of simple or supposedly simple sense perception we are increasingly discovering that the message which comes through the senses is itself mediated through a value system." [9] A good deal of the selectivity and concentration of observation arises from the value slant of the observer,

[9] Kenneth E. Boulding, *The Image* (Ann Arbor: University of Michigan Press, 1956, 1961), pp. 13-14.

either as this is aroused in the process or brought to the activity at inception. And if this slant sometimes causes distortion, leading him to see a lot of things that are not there, this need not happen. Indeed, where the value aim being pursued is pure knowledge or to observe simply to become aware of what is the case, the value slant becomes one of the major safeguards against distortion.

Besides a background of conation, a striving for ends and values, a cognitive background plays a large and even more evident role in observation. From the birth of consciousness we begin storage in memory of records that our observational machinery provides. These records not only expand continually, they modify subsequent observation. As language is acquired, families of concepts emerge, and competence in the established use of these concepts is developed by "a reinforcement supplied by the verbal community." [10] Individuals may reshape these concepts, but at any given time, it is sometimes claimed, "the concepts we have settle for us the form of the experience we have of the world." [11]

More precisely, of what is the cognitive background of observation constituted, and how does it function? In the preceding chapter I mentioned the cognitive a priori: the laws of logic or requirements of formal validity, and the principle of material necessity or the requirement of empirical truth. In observation these are necessities in knowledge insofar as the process is governed by the cognitive aim. They may have little effect in the activity of the undisciplined observer, but in fruitful observation their role is central. They form a kind of mind structure submerged

[10] B. F. Skinner, "The Operational Analysis of Psychological Terms," *Psychological Review*, vol. 52, 1945; reprinted in Herbert Feigl and May Brodbeck, *Readings in the Philosophy of Science* (New York: Appleton-Century-Crofts, 1953), p. 587.
[11] Peter Winch, *The Idea of a Social Science* (London: Routledge & Kegan Paul; New York: Humanities Press, 1958), p. 15.

in defective cognition but commanding in observation that fulfills the cognitive goal.

The cognitive background of observation, however, is far richer than its a priori principles. It has a "content" component, the accumulations of past cognitive activity: images, associations, memories of all sorts, including all of our retained formal learning. In the case of stored concepts and theories, our accumulations provide the individual and type identifications used in experiencing the things of our world. This occurs not merely in daily life but equally in the sciences. Here observation is often mediated by physical instruments that cannot be used intelligently without prior mastery of considerable theory. How can a person intelligently use a complicated instrument for measuring ionization if he does not know anything about the theory of ionization or even the established methods of scientific measurement? Such knowledge may serve numerous scientific purposes from the preparation of measuring instruments to the interpretation of observational results. But in instrument observation its prime role is to help us identify the instrument and the arrangement of its parts, and to focus attention upon what we should look with and what we should look for.

Besides sophisticating observation in this way, the content background can simplify it by supplying details that only much antecedent labor could otherwise furnish. In daily life, no less than in the sciences, this frequently happens. Glancing at a familiar copy of a book, we see at once that it is the missing volume we have been searching for. An unprepared observer, alert as he may be, would not see this at all. This simplification may occur in such marvelous ways that we may conclude, in the case of music for example, that we are actually hearing details which are only imagined, and we may fall into certain delusions. Jeans writes:

Many [loudspeakers of radios] are designed deliberately to cut out all frequencies below about 250, the frequency of about middle C, and so transmit no base or tenor tones at all. Yet we hear the double bass strings, the basses of the brass, and male voices with absolute clearness. The explanation is, of course, that all these sources of sound are rich in harmonics. Out of these our ears [*sic*] create the missing fundamental tones and lower harmonics as difference tones, and the combination of these with the higher harmonics, which come through unhindered, restores for us the tone played by the orchestra. Obviously this can only happen if the harmonics are transmitted in abundance.[12]

Thus, the cognitive background may not only enrich and simplify observation, but may also lead us to think we hear (or see) a great deal that is only imagined or suggested, thereby generating delusions. Yet ideas in this background referring to actualities transcending the observational actualities need not do this at all. In fact, they may complete the cognitive impulse originating an observation. The theoretic is of this sort. Indeed, it is a question whether fruitful observation can dispense with transobservational ideas. In the sciences, according to Lenzen, "all observation involves more or less explicitly the element of hypothesis."[13] In any case, observation can serve within larger ideas lodged in our cognitive background, and these ideas, far from deluding it, can give observation much greater cognitive scope.

This use in knowledge of transempirical ideas or ideas going beyond what is really experienced in observation indicates a whole new side of the cognitive enterprise, the theoretic, which we shall examine in the next chapter. It also raises certain questions about Empiricism as an epistemological theory, its meaning and limits.

[12] James Jeans, *Science and Music* (New York: Macmillan Co.; Cambridge: Cambridge University Press, 1937), p. 241.
[13] V. F. Lenzen, *Procedures of Empirical Science*, vol. 1, no. 5, *International Encyclopedia of Unified Science* (Chicago: University of Chicago Press, 1938), p. 4.

Empiricism

As a theory of knowledge, Empiricism is an account of
the origin and extent of knowledge, and proposes a criterion
or test for whatever claims to be knowledge. In modern
times, the classical statement of Empiricism is to be found
in Locke, Berkeley, and Hume. For Locke, experience
(cognitive experience) was inner and outer sensations.
These he called ideas, as did Berkeley (or at least Berkeley
called outer sensations ideas). Experience also was sensations for Hume, who, however, called them impressions,
reserving the term "idea" for a faded copy of an impression.
From this tradition blossomed the latter day sensa or sense-
data theory according to which experience is the awareness
of sense-quale—color, odor, sound, etc.—all of which
usually are considered private and subjective, as in traditional Empiricism.

I have already criticized the sense-data theory as a
theory of observation. But it has been subjected to adverse
criticism on additional grounds. Perhaps the most important recent criticisms of it have come from philosophers
of science. Ordinarily, they have noticed, when the scientist
talks science, he never talks about sense-data or his private
sensations. He talks about distances measured, movements
observed, apparatus, compounds, and other public items.
Only the psychologist studying sensations might normally
use the term "sensa" to refer to what he is talking about.
The "experience" on which scientists customarily base their
science seems very different from the "experience" described by the sense-data theory.

Moreover, the knowledge structures that comprise science seem incapable of being extracted from sense-data in
any combination. As Karl Popper writes: "Out of uninter-
rupted sense-experiences sciences cannot be distilled, no
matter how industriously we gather and sort them." [14] The

[14] Karl R. Popper, *The Logic of Scientific Discovery* (New York:
Science Editions, 1961), p. 280.

concept of an electron as significant in physical theory includes much more than any visual or other sensations we may have of it or of its photographic record. Indeed, no concept of consequence in physical science, light, heat, sound, motion, seems reducible without a considerable remainder to the sense-quale of anyone. And this is true of theories in science no less than concepts. "Classical mechanics is formulated as a set of differential equations, so that in consequence it is the 'instantaneous' coordinates of mechanical states that are required to be known in the application of the theory. However, instantaneous positions and momenta are never experimental data," [15] and certainly not sense-data in the meaning of the sense-data theory.

The conceptual and theoretical aspects of science thus raise certain problems for any empiricist theory of knowledge that retains the traditional concept of experience as awareness of private sensations. But setting aside this theory with its limitation of experience to the private and subjective, interpreting experience more broadly as confrontation of inner and outer "reality," as I have interpreted observation, how satisfactory are the answers of Empiricism to the questions of the origin, extent, and test of knowledge?

One may agree with the empiricist, as Kant did, that all knowledge begins *with* experience. But it does not follow, as Kant also pointed out, that knowledge therefore originates *from* experience. According to our view and Kant's, there is an a priori component equally necessary, and only from an awareness structured by this component, and not from a blank Lockean *tabula rasa,* does knowledge arise. The empirical is only one element accounting for the origin of knowledge.

[15] Ernest Nagel, *Freedom and Reason* (Glencoe, Ill.: Free Press, 1951), p. 252.

As to the extent of knowledge, I have already noted that observation or direct confrontation is limited to middle-sized entities. The vast regions of the subperceptual and superperceptual extend beyond it. Observation, of course, does provide considerable knowledge. What Popper has called "singular existential statements" (there is an *A* at *S-T*) are all "testable, intersubjectively, by 'observation'." [16] But these statements only begin to take us over the whole ground believed to be there for knowledge. Complex theories transcending observational limits are constantly needed to supplement them and overcome the perpetual if shifting limitations of empirical knowledge.

Finally, experience in itself is inadequate as the test of knowledge. Identification of things—"cat," "dog," "sky," —the singular existential statements of Popper, and similar elementary claims, seem testable by experience. In particular, theories seem falsifiable by noticing that the events they predict do not occur at the time or place or in the manner the theories predicted. But actually, in all these cases the test is not experience but the fulfillment or non-fulfillment of the cognitive aim. This background factor in observation is decisive, and experience serves merely as an instrument for determining whether the requirements of this aim in the given case have or have not been fulfilled. Indeed, no amount of experience that did not do this would lead us to accept a statement as knowledge. This point is reinforced when we leave the field of observation and project theories about objects beyond the middle-sized entities of our everyday world. It is the unified awareness that these theories give to all relevant details, this aim fulfillment, that inspires their birth and determines their survival in the domain of knowledge.

[16] Popper, *Logic,* p. 102.

Uses

Empiricism, then, fails as an adequate account of the origin, extent, and test of knowledge. Yet observation as cognitive experience informed by a priori factors is an extraordinary arm of knowledge with manifold uses.

For one thing, directed by a purely cognitive aim, it can provide a very impressive record of what is the case, of how things in confrontation look and act and react. This is especially true where observation is fortified by learning and training, and assisted by apparatus. In such activity, certain safeguards must be used. Just as we do not see the images on our retina in looking at a printed page, so our sensations and intuitions and other subjective components of observation are not ideas or objects in the Lockean sense. They are inner strands of the observational act and subject to aberration and distortion as any other observational instruments. Ordinarily, however, they can and do serve the ends of knowledge very competently. They can be obstructed. In Heisenberg's ideal experiment in quantum mechanics, observation is obstructed by the apparatus that must be used. By rendering indeterminate the value of one variable, such as the velocity of a particle, as one tries to determine the value of another variable, such as the position of the particle, the use of this apparatus results in "the essential impossibility of completely accurate observations."[17] Such physical frustration should induce additional caution in the cognitive claims made for observation. Still, it cannot cancel its considerable cognitive success.

This success gives observation a terminal value in the knowledge domain, or a value in its own right, independent of additional uses. But just because in so many cases it is such a superior source of information, observation has

[17] Moritz Schlick, *Philosophy of Nature* (New York: Philosophical Library, 1949), p. 69.

numerous instrumental values and uses. Roughly, these are of two sorts, noncognitive and cognitive.

The noncognitive is illustrated dramatically by the uses of observation for survival. Observation has served well in the long struggle for existence. It has steered human beings around what seem in retrospect appalling dangers and vicissitudes. This success has been primarily pragmatic, not cognitive, and has been sometimes accompanied by numerous superstitions. But it has also yielded considerable understanding of what things can do for man's weal and woe, and while observation is not the sole source of this understanding, it has been an almost continuous record of the bearings of the immediate physical and human environment on man's welfare.

An equally important illustration of the noncognitive use of observation is in technological production where it serves in the reshaping of inanimate and animate processes and materials. In technology, however, observation is only one of the cognitive resources employed instrumentally. Theory is also used in abundance, at least in modern technology. I shall therefore not enter into this subject at this point. But one remark might be made in passing. Heretofore technology in modern times has consisted chiefly in the application of natural science to observable physical processes and materials with results ranging from hearing aids to hydrogen bombs. We have seen, however, that in a sense observation can also bring the purposive behavior and values of human beings into its orbit. This suggests that technology, using observation as one means, might be capable of extending its operations to applications of normative knowledge to human beings, provided a body of theory regarding purposive behavior and norms comparable to our physical theory were established. I shall return to this topic in later chapters.

In cognition itself, the chief instrumental use of observation is to aid in the construction and testing of theories.

In testing, observation may verify that an event predicted by a theory occurred, and thus show that the theory is superior to some rival theory that did not allow this prediction or predicted the opposite. According to some, such observation "proves" the theory. Even careful scientists sometimes assert this. But what it proves is merely that the theory is superior to its rival. The argument "If X (theory), then Y (predicted event); but Y, therefore X," as any beginner in logic knows, far from proving X, commits the fallacy of affirming the consequent. Y can actually prove X, if at all, only where Y and X are equivalents: "If equilateral, then equiangular; but equiangular, therefore. . . ." Indeed, far from proving a theory, according to Popper's well-known thesis, the only logically justifiable role of observation in testing is the falsification of theory.[18] When observation shows us that predicted consequences do not occur, or that events contradicting the predicted consequences do occur, it enables us to discard a theory and thus simplify the theoretical structure of science. Such falsification of theory is certainly a necessary part of the growth of knowledge, and the role of observation in many cases of theory falsification is indispensable.

Even if observation of verifying events does not logically prove a theory, it has considerable cognitive significance. It has the obvious psychological value of increasing our confidence in a theory so verified. Indeed, observation generally may have a number of important psychological values for an inquirer. For example, it may stimulate memory and imagination. A person may approach a problem with no explicit idea of how to solve it. By looking over the situation, observing exactly what is there, he may leap quickly to an effective solution, or set up a theory that the

[18] Popper, *Logic*, chap. 1, sec. 6; chap. 4.

mind can canvas as a very valuable preliminary to a solution. Popper holds that this operation of the mind, usually called induction, has no more than psychological significance.[19] In induction, you observe some part or parts of a situation and leap to an idea that seems to illumine the whole or you observe one or more instances of a phenomenon and jump to the conclusion that all instances are so-and-so. In either type of induction, your leap or jump is not logically founded. The characteristics of a part or parts, or of one instance or several, are not necessarily the characteristics of wholes or all instances, as experience shows. Hence, your inductive leap is a step beyond the evidence, and logically insecure. Nor does the uniformity of nature principle remedy this defect, as Hume noted long ago. The uniformity principle is itself a generalization that, as applying to the whole of nature, goes far beyond observational evidence and is open to the same criticism as any inductive generalization and suffers from the same logical insecurity.

All this, the logical inconclusiveness and insecurity of induction, may be granted. Yet one may feel that something has been left out. Induction may logically be a leap into the dark. But does this reduce its cognitive importance to only psychological value? Epistemologically, it remains an effort to tie in our accumulated observations and knowledge with the unknown, and widen the horizons of awareness. And in some cases it does this with remarkable boldness and incisiveness, setting up theoretical structures that often modify the whole incline and system of knowledge. Newton observing an apple fall, Watt watching a kettle of water boil, Roentgen discovering some fogged photographic plates—these abstractly trivial observations generated theories that gave an extraordinarily enlarged unity to our awareness of the way things are. The Baconian conception of induction—according to which a passive

[19] Popper, *Logic*, chap. 1,

blank mind reads off a generalization about the form of a phenomenon by examining a tripartite table listing a few score particular unanalyzed experiments—is only a very imperfect description of what actual induction involves. There are background accumulations, multitudes of anticipations, live experimental observations, to be sure. But above all there is the epistemological purpose that informs the inductive act. This is the effort to use what we know to understand what we do not yet know, and by a process of synthesis to enlarge the frontiers of awareness of the world that is there to be known. In this, induction is carrying forward the true intent of the cognitive act and the basic aim of theory construction.

III

Theory Construction

Observation and Theory

Much cognition seems to terminate with observation. In our earliest years and in mature life we record endless details that we do not use and that pass from available memory before we think of using them. We know we knew many of them—how a certain wall in Rome looked at ten o'clock on the morning of the fifteenth of March in 1938. But we cannot now recall at all this momentary record. Nonrecall, however, is not the essential mark of observationally terminal cognition. A dancer may learn the steps of a new ballet not from theoretical explanations, but simply by watching the steps being demonstrated by the instructor. This visual knowledge may persist, and be recalled several times. But it may be otherwise unused, and in recall not exceed the initial recording.

This account of our observational knowing, it may be said, is really very superficial. After all, each symbol that sprouts in consciousness occurs within a mind and is connected with the systematic understanding that forms the grasp of the world of this mind. Integration with a larger symbolic system occurs as symbols form, and in this respect symbolization in observation is no exception. Also, each of us colors his knowing with the quality of his personality. An eclectic and an original mind will integrate details differently, each exhibiting the stamp of his personality. All knowing is personal knowing,[1] and not just a mechanical depersonalized recording like the action of a camera.

These two points—the integration in the mind of observational knowledge, and its personal quality—seem perfectly acceptable in our account, and are herewith accepted. But they should not obscure two other points. First, observational knowledge is a distinct kind of knowledge. Consequently, in cognition it may be the end aimed at or the only end attained. In these cases, observational knowing may be properly described as terminal cognition although it is integrated in the mind as it occurs with our other epistemic accumulations. Second, personality may color our observational knowledge, but in usual instances observation is more than its personal colorings. It purports to disclose the things of the world, and its claim to be making an object-disclosure can usually be tested and is often found acceptable though it is sometimes rejected. There is much more to observational knowledge as knowledge than its personal quality.

It would certainly be misleading to say, however, that observing consists only, or primarily, of terminal cognitions. Indeed, usually observation is a step on the way to the fulfillment of a larger aim. In innumerable situations it does not give us all we want, and we seek to press beyond it. An urgent elementary need such as an infant's hunger moves it to explore beyond what it is touching at the time, and to plunge into the unobserved. This is a crude parallel on the sensory level of the theory impulse. What we see and hear is not enough to give us the answers we seek. More is needed. We must probe beyond the observed. Such

[1] Cf. Michael Polanyi, *Personal Knowledge* (London: Routledge & Kegan Paul, 1958; Chicago: University of Chicago Press, 1958, 1962).

a cognitive effort to fill out the whole needed to satisfy the aim in motion draws heavily, of course, on observational fact and memory. But it is an endeavor different from observation, and builds up a different type of memory. When it matures in the trained knower, it rests upon a structure of transobservational principles of great range and interpretive power.

Natural science supplies abundant illustrations of these principles. "Science progresses, not by recognizing the truth of new observations alone, but by making sense of them. To this task of interpretation we bring principles of regularity, conceptions of natural order, paradigms, ideals, or what-you-will: intellectual patterns which define the range of things we can accept (in Copernicus' phrase) as 'sufficiently absolute and pleasing to the mind'." [2] These patterns defining our range of intellectual tolerance may at any time become too narrow in some respects, and need recasting. In full being they consist of what we have called the a priori in knowledge together with those theoretical principles historically developed that have been capable of reaching beyond observation to that distance that the cognitive aim in the situations investigated seems to have required. It is from this base, in whole or part, that new theoretical projections are made in natural science, "no inquiry being possible without some conceptual scheme." [3] And what is true of natural science is true of history, philosophy, or everyday life. In philosophy, for example, we may be said to begin with wonder. But it is a very sophisticated wonder, a Socratic wonder whose background may be as extensive as the region of Platonic Ideas. "Philosophy," says Ortega, "represents the greatest impulse toward an integrated whole within the intellectual

[2] Stephen Toulmin, *Foresight and Understanding* (Bloomington: Indiana University Press, 1961), p. 81.
[3] Willard V. Quine, *Word and Object* (Cambridge, Mass.: M.I.T. Press, 1960), p. 4.

sphere," [4] and fulfilling this impulse in any degree seems possible only with a large theoretic background that includes cognizance of theory in the sciences and other areas where observation is vital yet insufficient.

The cognitive insufficiency of observation and the requisite role of theory in knowledge does not mean that we approach every situation in science or philosophy or elsewhere with a ready-made hypothesis about its problematic features. Often, especially in everyday situations, we meet no problem at all. When we do, it may baffle us completely; we may have no hypothesis at all to offer. Even in advanced sciences, investigation by no means always follows the Popper model of empirically testing preconceived theory. Much of it, from Einstein's formulation of his theory of relativity to the discovery of a "miracle" drug such as penicillin, follows the more conventional model of beginning with observations, sometimes other people's observations (Michelson's and Morley's, for example) whose results are discordant with existing belief, and attempting to restore the wholeness of view disrupted by the clash of these observations with existing belief. The settled theoretical background in a field is frequently unprepared to illumine the novelties encountered in later experience. It needs reconstruction, transformation, growth. And it needs this not necessarily because the world is changing or growing, but because this theoretical background was designed to overcome observational discordances in situations different from the new ones now being faced.

In such circumstances, the first business of theory is not to change the world but to change itself so that with observation it will help us to see the world as it is. If a remark of Wittgenstein's, "Philosophy leaves everything as it was," [5] is interpreted in a certain way, we can say that

[4] Jose Ortega y Gasset, *Meditations on Quixote*, trans. Evelyn Rugg and Diego Marin (New York: Norton & Co., 1963), p. 38.
[5] Winch, *Idea of a Social Science*, p. 103.

all knowing leaves everything as it was. The things we make theories about, stars and gases no less than our neighbor's intentions, are assumed in cognition to be as they are whether our theories are true or false. We grant them an ontological independence, objective items in manifold world relations, and in our theories we try to depict these things as they are in this independent state. We do not try to change them spatially, temporally, or in general ontologically, in cognition. Or if we do change them in this way we are likely to regard the process of knowing as frustrated as in the Heisenberg ideal experiment, or we are intent on knowing the things not as they are, but as undergoing the introduced changes.

Yet this passivity or ontological ineffectuality of theory construction can easily be misunderstood. Theory construction is not passive picture-taking. It is a creative process. Observation itself, we have seen, is not altogether innocent of creativity. In observation at its best, eyes and ears, nerves, brain, and consciousness itself are servants of otherness, bent on recording the object correctly. But this record is made in terms of the observer's resources, his symbols and capacities, and he produces his version of what is the case—an individuated novelty that did not exist before then. With theory construction creativity has still greater range. The lacunae of observation must be filled, sometimes requiring a great imaginative synthesis. As in observation so in theory: the theory of the atom for example, this conceptual creation, like a work of art, may conspicuously take on the color and quality of the creator's personality.

To anyone who knew the bluff colonial manner of Rutherford, the roughness and the twinkle, the solemn sense of pulling his own leg, everything in his discovery of the structure of the atom is of a piece. The metaphors are as much a part of Rutherford's personality as the idea of the experiment. They all have the thumb print of a man to whom the core of things had a strong

and clear outline—even if it was as minute as the nucleus—and
who judged things by tests which had to be equally clear and
strong. Everything here is as individual and human as Rembrandt. Do you remember the pictures of his mistress that
Rembrandt painted as an old man and that no one would buy?
They have the same obstinate tangle of feelings, rough and
tender at the same time, that Rutherford had for his mistress,
nature.[6]

To be sure, the purposes of creative imagination in art and
in science are different. Art wishes to show things in a certain way. Whether these things are independently that way
is usually not its chief concern. On the other hand, in
science this is of capital concern.[7] The independent world
cannot be ignored. "Man proposes . . . Nature disposes."[8]
This fate awaits all scientific theory.

Theory sometimes requires great imaginative syn-
theses. Imagination here is creative imagination, the power
to connect the previously separated and disconnected, the
absent and the present, and produce a new idea. "In Octo-
ber 1833," Darwin writes, "I happened to read for amuse-
ment Malthus on Population, and being well prepared to
appreciate the struggle for existence which everywhere
goes on from long continued observation of the habits of
animals and plants, it at once struck me that under these
circumstances favorable variations would tend to be pre-
served, and unfavorable ones to be destroyed. The result
of this would be the formation of new species. Here then
I had a theory by which to work."[9] No doubt not all
examples of successful imaginative synthesis in science are

[6] J. Bronowski, "The Abacus and the Rose," *Nation*, vol. 198, no. 1,
Jan. 4, 1964, p. 13.
[7] D. W. Gotshalk, *Art and the Social Order* (New York: Dover Publications, 1962). Chap. 2 develops this contrast; chap. 1 develops the
contrast between aesthetic and cognitive experience.
[8] R. B. Braithwaite, *Scientific Explanation* (Cambridge: Cambridge
University Press, 1959), p. 368.
[9] William C. Dampier, *A History of Science* (Cambridge: Cambridge
University Press; New York: Macmillan Co., 1946), p. 295.

as simple and straightforward as this of Darwin combining his own observations of animals and plants with Malthus' discussion of population to produce a new idea of the machinery of species evolution. But the example I believe contains the major rudiments of even the most complex theory construction.

Creative Factors

The emergence of the theory impulse in the life of the individual, and the growth of the various forms it may take from the first prelingual cognitive reachings beyond immediate awareness to the most sophisticated structures in science and philosophy is a problem of formidable scope for genetic psychology. I shall not attempt to investigate the problem here but shall be content with the more modest task of enumerating the factors that at a minimum seem necessary for the occurrence of theory in its most generally recognized form. These creative factors are four: data, individual insight, cognitive aim, and background value system.

The data are any accumulations of observation and theory relevant to the situation eliciting the theory and assumed to be usable as a basis for solving the problem at hand. In different situations these "givens" will vary. One may pile up immense amounts of data about a situation yet not seem to have enough, while sometimes a few elementary observations and a discussion in a book may be all that is needed. The chief certainties about the data are that they define what the knower believes he knows about the situation, his unproblematic awareness, and they do not add up. They pose but do not solve the problem. They present the facts, as the theorist believes he knows these facts, but they await a leap of the imagination to be functioning alive in the solution of the problem.

Until this second factor, the imaginative leap, occurs,

nothing theoretic that is new or creative has entered into the problematic situation. The term "new" here must be taken in a very relative sense. The imaginative leap may consist of no more than applying in a new context a well-known idea, as when Dalton revived in modern times the ancient theory of atoms. Indeed, there is probably no theory so novel that it is not analogous in some very general way to an idea fairly familiar and even of long ancestry. Still, where a theory is proposed that comes to be regarded as a genuine addition to knowledge, it is new in at least two respects. Cognitively it goes beyond the recognized situational data, and brings in an idea exceeding this data in cognitive power and range. Second, where it consists of using an already established idea, it is not a merely routine application of this idea but in some perceptible way extends the scope that the idea had had up to that time.

This imaginative leap in theory formation I have called individual insight. This label suggests that theory construction is the work of the individual knower and bears the hallmarks of the individual. It also suggests that what is called "team research" is not itself a virtue except as it heightens the stimulation available to its indivduals. All this is true, but in the end secondary. The chief reference of "individual" in the present connection is to another character of the emerging cognition. Whether the problem is to reconcile two theories, classical mechanics and Maxwellian electromagnetics, or whether it is to produce an idea that could deductively generate the diverse data of all pertinent observation or in some other way exceed the given, the primary goal of the imaginative leap is to organize diversity into unity, to individuate the epistemic multiplicity so that it is connected into a single, unitary, and more comprehensive symbolic system. "The central problem of epistemology," Popper writes, "has always been and

still is the problem of the growth of knowledge." [10] In a
negative way this is assisted by discarding disproved
theory—simplifying by negation the region of possibilities.
But in a positive way the great step in this growth is to
overcome recalcitrant diversity and to extend the province
of intelligible unity. And this sort of enlarged individua-
tion of awareness is what the imaginative leap of the
theorist tries to do and actually does do in successful instances of theory construction.

The imaginative leap of the theorist has some aim behind it, a cognitive drive. This aim or drive, the third
creative factor, might be described as an effort to increase
situational awareness coherently. In its widest reaches in
natural science it yields "a sense of the unity of nature," [11]
and in philosophy a sense of the unity of the universe. But
in most cases its result is much more limited. The theorist
is immersed in a restricted puzzling situation. With the intellectual resources in his possession, he is incapable of
coming to an unpuzzling understanding of it. Some additional cognitive device must be invented. This is theory,
and the test of theory in this context is that it contain or
imply what would enable the knower to realize the requisites of unified awareness in the situation. All symbolic
elements necessary for this purpose must be included.

The fourth creative factor that should be added to
data, individual insight, and cognitive aim, to complete the
list of minimum formative elements, is the value system of
the theorist. Even in pursuit of the purest knowledge where
the overwhelming aim is simply to know, a value system
functions. For if the theorist did not prize pure knowledge,
would he pursue it? Boulding writes: "A considerable part

[10] Popper, *Logic*, p. 15.
[11] Bronowski, "The Abacus and the Rose," p. 10.

of the success of the scientific community in advancing knowledge must be attributed to its value system in which an impersonal devotion to truth is regarded as the highest value to which both personal and national pride must be subordinated." [12] In regard to theory, the point may be stated more specifically by noting that all theory is selective. It is a theory of "this" rather than "that." The reasons for the selection may range from pure cognitive interest to personal or professional ambition. But whatever they are, these reasons embody ends that the theorist hopes his theory will serve and whose attainment the theorist values. This coloring of knowledge by value seems inevitable so long as a theorist has any purpose in theorizing. Moreover, it seems basic since it connects knowledge with conation and the dynamism of the human enterprise. The positivist's dream of a value-free knowledge does not seem realizable unless the human knower is converted into a pure fact-recording machine. But even "pure" fact, if cognitive, is a myth, for a fact in knowledge is valuable for something: a building block for theory or a check on it. Were facts of no use at all—some are almost that—they would be discarded and not prized as they are. It is because "fact" has "value" or potential "value" written over its face that it has recognized stature in knowledge.

All this, as I have indicated previously, does not mean the necessary corruption or distortion of knowledge by alien elements. Value may distort. Wishful thinking may invade cognition with unfortunate consequences. But the personality and value inclinations of a theorist may color his results without distortion. The economy and precision, the smoothness and accuracy a theorist prizes may be displayed in his results, and far from detracting from

[12] Kenneth E. Boulding, *The Meaning of the Twentieth Century* (New York: Harper & Row, 1964), p. 45.

their cognitive quality, these personal attributes and values may greatly enhance the results as knowledge.[13]

Rationalism

Theory construction, as I have described it, is a kind of taking up of data into a larger symbolic form designed in a puzzling situation to meet the cognitive demand there for a unitary comprehensive awareness. If reason is defined, as it sometimes is, as the power to maximize some quantity, such as cognitive grasp, theory construction, as I have described it, would seem to be the work of the purest reason, and the great triumphs of theory in our most advanced sciences would seem to be incontrovertible testimony to the sovereignty of reason in knowledge.

This view brings up the doctrine of Rationalism. In its classical modern form, Rationalism is the theory that pure reason is the source, the test and the determiner of the extent of knowledge. Experience is incompetent to be any of these things. Indeed, the great role of experience in knowledge is to present problems, and supply experimental data to reason for judging solutions. And if, in verification, experience seems to give us solutions, this is because reason there has decided that these are solutions and not irrelevant to the theory it has proposed. This is a very rough short summary of the classical Rationalist doctrine, at least as it is found in Descartes's *Meditations* and *Discourse on Method.*

While a case for Rationalism as a theory of knowledge thus seems possible, it is not difficult to see that this case is imperfect. Rationalism cannot give us wholly satisfactory answers to the major epistemological questions of the origin, test, and extent of knowledge.

Our primordial awareness of the world, the beginnings

[13] Gotshalk, *Patterns of Good and Evil,* chaps. 6 and 7. Cf. L. S. Vygotsky, *Thought and Language,* trans. E. Hanfmann and G. Vakar (Cambridge, Mass.: M.I.T. Press, 1962), p. 8.

of knowledge, is not an act of pure reason. It is an immediate experience informed by structural features of the mind but accomplished by our bodily organs and senses. Knowledge begins not with reason but with structured experience. It is here that our first intimations of the way things are dawn upon us. As knowledge grows, it is true, rational theory outstrips the range of available experience. But new experience may open up territory not intelligible on present theory, and so be as vital in determining the extent of knowledge as successful rational theory. Although the principles of wholeness of view and maximum intelligibility may be credited to reason, and function as master criteria in testing cognitions and determining their knowledge properties, still an objective check also is imperative, both in the natural sciences and in everyday life. No pure abstractly coherent view is enough. A coherent view *of the situational diversity* is necessary, and ingress into this diversity ordinarily can be accomplished only by empirical awareness.

What appears to fit almost without remainder into the rationalistic theory is not the knowledge we have in natural science and everyday life, but formal systems in which the entities are freely constructed and the rules of formation and transformation are freely stipulated, as mathematical systems are sometimes said to be. Such systems seem to originate from pure reason working according to its own law of formal coherence and seeking maximum extension of its formal possibilities. But even here some qualifications appear to be necessary. These systems are late and sophisticated developments. They would hardly be possible without antecedent experience in handling symbols. A person must be familiar with "2" and "addition" before he can hope to chart a new area of higher arithmetic. He gains this familiarity first as a child, learning these terms as he learns "cat" or "book," through instances observed in experience. Moreover, these constructed systems are significant as knowledge in revealing the principles of formal systems in maximum range. Thereby, they provide not merely a purely rational knowledge but also insight into what natural science and everyday knowledge can be on their formal side, if there is an empirical occasion for them to use any of these new formal systems.

Rationalism as an answer to the problems of the theory of knowledge, then, seems capable of only a very imperfect confirmation. Its strongest claim in the domain of knowledge, I think, is in its criterion for testing ideas. This is a truly universal criterion, even though for much knowledge, such as natural science, it is not sufficient. In knowledge, in other words, the main role of reason is normative. It is a guide and direction-giver. In theory construction imagination is the originator. It connects ideas so as to produce a new idea. But it is guided in successful construction by the rational aim of maximum coherence, and in all such cases the guidance of reason seems an indispensable factor in the orderly advance of theory. Owing to this fact many of the great early modern theorists such as Copernicus, cautiously seeking new paths in the knowledge domain, were very strongly inclined toward Rationalism.

In addition to giving considerable scope to the exercise of reason, theory construction has other uses. It will help us to place it more exactly in the domain of knowledge to describe a few of these uses.

Uses of Theory

The general function of theory in knowledge is to annex territory to the intelligible world. By awareness of the directly encountered, observation does this in its own way. But as even elementary practical needs show, much remains to be done, and theory tries to accomplish what more is needed.

In the creation of formal systems, theory construction seems to produce regions of intelligibility out of the whole cloth. In ideal languages, in mathematics as sometimes interpreted, the terms of the system have only the properties assigned to them and may be combined only according to the postulates and rules stipulated. The result is a pure theoretic structure, antecedently nonexistent, new, yet intelligible throughout. Here theory has mapped a region of possibility and added it to the other areas of knowledge. If it is dependent in this on an imagination prepared by prior experience of actuality and especially of symbols, it has transcended its ancestry in its results.

Besides mapping regions of possibility, theory is used to chart large areas of actuality. One of the most important instances of this is the construction of laws in natural science. "Generally speaking, the formulation of a law concerning any natural process consists in stating the *particular combination* (function) of those variable magnitudes or quantities describing the process *which remain constant during the whole process*,"[14] e.g., Galileo's laws of acceleration, Newton's law of gravitation. Sometimes, the term "natural law" is used to mean regularities or recurrences actually in nature. In this sense natural laws are not the handiwork of theory. But in natural science law also means the description of such regularities or the theoretic formulation of their features. In this sense the formulation of law in natural science is part of the theoretic enterprise, an effort to contribute to our knowledge a unified symbolization of events. Laws are theories about order in nature, which attempt to give an account of the patterns of persistent quantities to be found there: "Physical theories provide patterns within which data appear intelligible. They constitute a 'conceptual Gestalt'."[15]

[14] Schlick, *Philosophy of Nature*, p. 20. Italics and parentheses his.
[15] Hanson, *Patterns of Discovery*, p. 90.

In scientific law so understood, theory is used first of all for description. It is initially an attempt to depict patterns to be found among quantities and events in nature. In the mathematically more advanced natural sciences, however, these formulations often are "idealized" to simplify the mathematics. They are descriptions to which nature only approximates. But such formulae are correctable in application by allowing for the deviant conditions of the natural situation. In natural science law is also used for explanation, to supply the rationale of events. In this context law is sometimes distinguished from theory. Law is defined as the formulation of invariable regularities found in the experience we have: "We only try to find laws that will order the experience we have." [16] Laws are not theories. Boyle's law is not a theory but merely an ordering of observations. On the other hand, to explain laws, natural science uses not higher laws but theories. Theories are higher generalities by which natural science through deductive procedures explains its laws. Thus, "from the [molecular] theory of gases we can deduce the laws [of gases, such as Boyle's]." [17]

The chief differences between this view and our own is terminological. There may be a substantive point at stake. Unlike summaries, at least as ordinarily understood, laws in natural science usually have a generality of application exceeding the observations we have made. In particular, they are commonly valued for their predictive power. They imply something about the future and the elsewhere, while summaries are limited strictly to events that have occurred in our present and past. However this may be, the chief point is that, besides description, theory is used as explanation. In our sense of law, theory explains obser-

[16] Norman Campbell, *What Is Science?* (New York: Dover Publications, 1952), p. 69.
[17] Campbell, *What Is Science?*, p. 82.

vational facts: Boyle's law explains the measurements of pressure and volume found in the observation of gases. In Campbell's sense of law, theory explains laws: the molecular theory explains Boyle's law of gases.

Perhaps the chief mode of explanation furnished by theory in the natural sciences is as a deductive base of natural knowledge. It may be an observed event that needs explanation, or a set of empirical laws, Kepler's laws of celestial mechanics and Galileo's laws of terrestrial mechanics, which Newton explained by his law of gravitation. In any case, some segment or segments of natural knowledge present a puzzle in some respects. They raise questions: specifically, why are they as they are? Theory shows the segment or segments to be part of a larger pattern, included in a more comprehensive scheme. An empirical law is explained by discovering a broader conception from which it is a deduction, and "an event is explained . . . when it is shown to be part of an intelligible pattern of events." [18]

Theory, however, may explain in various other ways. It may explain by identification. Given the cellular theory, a certain color configuration under a microscope may be explained by identifying it as the nucleus of a cell. In much the same way, a theory may explain by classification. On a current theory, an entity in nature may be explained as a plant and not an animal. Again, theory may explain by analysis. It may explain a mental state, a Lockean complex idea, a Freudian complex, by analyzing out the "simple" factors said to have generated it. Or theory may explain by analogy. It may explain sound as a wave phenomenon by the analogy of the waves propagated on the smooth surface of a lake by a pebble thrown into the water.

But by far the most powerful way theory explains in natural science, and, in the view of some, the only really

[18] Hanson, *Patterns of Discovery*, p. 94.

important way, to which all other useful methods can be reduced, is as a deductive base. Theory here supplies a framework of fundamental ideas that gives intelligibility to observational data and empirical laws by showing them to be consequences of its premises. The high stature of this explanatory use of theory in natural science is shown by the fame attaching to the inventors of the more comprehensive of these systematic conceptions. "The greatest fame is reserved for those who conceive new frameworks of fundamental ideas, and so integrate apparently disconnected branches of science. Isaac Newton, Clerk Maxwell, and Charles Darwin are best remembered not as great experimenters or observers, but as critical and imaginative creators of new intellectual systems." [19] In this type of explanatory enterprise theory can reach its cognitive maximum by attempting to bring under its account the whole of nature. Thus did Democritus try with his theory of atoms and the void, and Einstein with his unified field theory.[20]

To description and explanation in natural science one should add the use of theory for prediction. Whether this is one of the major uses of theory in science, as Braithwaite believes,[21] or whether it is merely incidental to the chief purpose of describing the order of nature, as Toulmin contends,[22] I shall not debate. But in the sciences, and also in everyday life, theory customarily has a range far beyond observational data, implying features that should appear in unexamined situations, future, past, and present. This gives it predictive power. Illustrations of this power are

[19] Toulmin, *Foresight and Understanding*, p. 109.
[20] On explanation in natural science, besides Campbell, Braithwaite, Schlick, Hanson, Toulmin, see: J. H. Woodger, *Biological Principles* (London: Routledge & Kegan Paul, 1919, 1948); A. C. Benjamin, *The Logical Structure of Science* (London: Routledge & Kegan Paul, 1936); Warren Weaver, "Scientific Explanation," *Science*, vol. 143, March 20, 1964, pp. 1297-1300.
[21] Braithwaite, *Scientific Explanation*, p. 239.
[22] Toulmin, *Foresight and Understanding*, p. 36 ff.

profuse and require no detailed mention. They range from predicting an eclipse on the basis of observations and a theory of celestial mechanics to forecasting a politician's next move on the basis of observation of his past actions and a theory of his character and motives.

The uses of theory just enumerated—description, explanation, prediction—are, as I have indicated, particularly prominent in the empirical sciences. Probably it is going too far to say with Popper that "the empirical sciences are systems of theories." [23] These sciences also contain a sizable arsenal of observational data. But in the empirical sciences the use of theory to describe, explain, and predict must necessarily be very extensive. The scope of direct observation even enhanced by the most sensitive instruments is limited compared with the apparently vast microscopic and macroscopic dimensions of the universe now open to inference.

However, such exemplary cognitive uses of theory by no means exhaust its utility. As many know only too well, theory has had spectacular use in technology. Prediction and control are sometimes said to be the supreme aims of modern science,[24] and the control of natural materials and processes that the insights of scientific theory make possible is the foundation of modern technology. This transcognitive use of scientific theory raises several questions of far-reaching importance for our account of knowledge, but chiefly these: has the emphasis in the technological use of scientific theory in modern times been the right emphasis? An unfortunate emphasis? What are the full possibilities of the technological application of scientific knowledge? These questions will be raised again and discussed in Chapters VII and VIII. Before considering them, I want to focus on other details of the domain of knowledge.

[23] Popper, *Logic*, p. 59.
[24] E. A. Burtt, "The Value of Presuppositions of Science," *Bulletin of the Atomic Scientists*, vol. 13, no. 3, March, 1957, p. 101.

The Four Components

In the broadest sense of the term, the theoretic includes the general assumptions we bring to a situation, as well as the fresh explicit inferences or projections we make to resolve the puzzles of a situation. The theoretic is that total arc of the cognitive process that goes beyond observational data to try to complete the requirements of awareness. In this sense of theory, observation and theory construction might be said to constitute all of the process of the domain of knowledge. (Like the use of instruments, I regard experimentation in science or elsewhere as a method of broadening the field of observation rather than as an independent cognitive operation.) Knowledge is awareness of what is the case. Where observation does not give us this, theory seeks to give it, and where theory and observation do not give it, it is not attained.

The combination of acts, observation and theory construction, functions in daily life as in specialized research, and in the knowledge of everyday purposive acts as in that of recondite mechanical processes. The scientist feels the pressure of a gas on his hand, and infers the bombardment of a vast array of particles. A person sees the sulk on his friend's face, and infers resentment in his friend at a remark just made. Often our greatest convictions about what we know are about other people, their attitudes and responses, not about the hidden mechanics of physical existence. Usually the acts producing these convictions begin with observation and complete themselves in inference. A theoretical projection, issuing from a wealth of past knowledge and continuing assumptions, occurs at or after the moment of observation. Nor is the projection in regard to human beings intrinsically less reliable than the projection in regard to physical existence. All depends on the situation, especially the qualifications of the projector.

In the domain of knowledge, besides the processes of observation and theory construction, there is the result of these processes: the knowledge achieved. This result is complex. But I think it can be analyzed into four major components. The first is symbols, the material component. The second is the order given to the symbols, the formal component. The third is the unity of view that the symbols so ordered provide. The fourth is the functions or ends that symbolic arrays with a unity of view serve or can serve. In summary, in any successful result of the cognitive processes, one can distinguish the materials composing it, the form in which these materials are arrayed, the enlightenment that these arrayed materials give, and the function this enlightenment performs or can perform.

Having now given an account of the processes of knowing in this and the preceding chapter, I propose, in the next four chapters, to discuss *seriatim* these four components of the product of knowing, thereby completing the analysis of what goes on and what is accomplished in the domain of knowledge.

IV

The Materials of Knowledge

Varieties

The term "materials of knowledge" is ambiguous. It may mean the matter being cognized, as the earth in geology. It may mean the notes and apparatus used in an investigation. It may mean the internal fabric of knowledge. In my usage, "materials of knowledge" will have only this last meaning. It will refer to the "stuff" composing knowledge. This stuff, I have said, is symbols. Expressing a commonly held view of symbolic functioning and symbols, Whitehead writes: "The human mind is functioning symbolically when some components of its experience elicit consciousness, beliefs, emotions, and usages, respecting other components of its experience." [1]

As the materials of knowledge, perhaps the first thing to note about symbols is their considerable variety. We tend to think of knowledge as statements in books, and statements as words, and words as the elementary components of knowledge. But actually words and statements are limited and rather recondite types of symbols. The original

[1] Alfred North Whitehead, *Symbolism: Its Meaning and Effect* (New York: Macmillan Co., 1927; G. P. Putnam's Sons, Capricorn Books, 1955), pp. 7-8.

symbolizing materials are psychological. Sensations, intuitions, feelings are cognitions of otherness, registering in the knower elements of his world. To be sure, they are not merely cognitions. Sensations and feelings, for example, may excite us to run, to wait, to deliberate, to do many things. But as cognitions, in addition to existing, they record other things as in existence—colors, sounds, shapes, danger—and so stand in our being for the being of others.

Beyond these primitive symbols the human being possesses a vast arsenal of other symbols that amplify awareness in a variety of ways. Many of these are alingual, even prelingual—hand gestures and body movements and pantomime, tones of voice, contact pressures.[2] Even before we can use words or without the use of words, any of these may come to signify what we know or want, or what state we are in. Physical events may become symbols. Clouds may signify rain, and rain at a certain time and place may signify that autumn is setting in. Indeed, to the imaginative, such as a Bishop Berkeley, the whole of physical nature may become a vast book of symbols.

The evolution of our symbolic repertoire from primitive awareness to the most sophisticated symbols of the advanced sciences is a problem of genetic psychology into which again I shall not enter except to say that at various points in human growth not only natural events such as rain and fire are added to man's symbolic repertoire, but also artificial entities such as words, mathematical signs, and musical notes. These artificial additions are expanded and refined, and generate an awareness of the greatest range and complexity. In certain respects, they represent the maximum in symbolic subtlety and power so far attained by man in his cognitive materials. We shall want

[2] Ayer, in *The Problem of Knowledge*, p. 12, notes: "A dog knows its master, a baby knows its mother, but they do not know any statements to be true."

to scan these entities from time to time to understand further the considerable variety of cognitive materials.

Meaning

A symbol is commonly said to have meaning, or to be an existent that means. But "meaning" like "materials" is an ambiguous term. First of all, one can distinguish two very broad senses of meaning—a value and a cognitive sense. In the statement "I did not know X meant so much to you," the term "meant" is the equivalent of "had so much value." Except where explicitly indicated, this sense of meaning will not be used in our discussion. I shall limit meaning to its cognitive use. In this sense, meaning can be analyzed in various ways. A very common way is to analyze it into denotation and connotation, reference and description. The term "table" means, denotes, refers to a piece of furniture, and means, connotes, describes furniture with certain characteristics.

Some symbols are said to have connotation but no denotation—a perfect circle with no exemplification in nature. Other symbols are said to have denotation but no connotation—a proper name such as Socrates. But to a person who knew Socrates personally, or even from Plato's *Dialogues*, the term "Socrates" probably would come to mean not only an individual man but a man with numerous extraordinary characteristics. As knowledge increases and our acquaintance with individuals deepens, this would appear to be true of proper names generally. As to perfect circles, characters in fiction, and the like, it may be the case that they do not denote anything in nature. But they do denote definite and even individual objects of awareness. In pure mathematics, as the saying is, we do not know what we are talking about or whether what we say is true, so far as the natural world goes. But we do know what a mathematical system would apply to, namely, to any field of entities that exhibited the properties assigned in the postulates. A field of denotation is indicated although one may not be able to produce an instance in nature at the moment. This is true in fiction and the fine arts. No doubt the extraordinary wealth of suggestive or descriptive content in the best works, along with the marvelous way this wealth is ordered so that it seems complete and satisfying in itself, excludes the possibility of the full identification of the entities in these creations with things in physical nature or in everyday life. Fine art can soar into a region of pure imagination that romantics seem to believe is its true home. Such imaginative creations, however, in representational art but even in nonrepresentational, do give us definite objects to which their descriptive content applies. These objects, like Alice in Wonderland, are as definite to imagination as the most immediate natural objects are to sensation. Denotation is not lacking, indeed it is often very precise, but it is different from the denotation of physical and everyday terms.

It is more important perhaps to question the view that denotation and connotation consist of such standard references and descriptions as found in a dictionary. Such a view even of verbal symbols vastly impoverishes the meaning of meaning. So much of what is meant by many statements in everyday life is not to be found in the most sophisticated word books. A sentence intoned in a certain way in a certain context by an intimate friend may communicate meanings to which a dictionary can give only the slightest clue. A single word, a baby's "Mama," may speak volumes about what is wanted or convey information about all sorts of other things. The explicit descriptions assigned to symbols in dictionaries usually are only an abstract fragment of their full connotation in live contexts. In the sciences this great amplitude of meaning is often lost since the chief interest is in generality rather than intimacy of understanding. But it abounds in everyday life, and can appear in science, for example, a cry of discovery characteristic of a fellow investigator occurring during his work.

Our enlargement of the field of denotation beyond the physical world to include any object of cognitive attention, imaginary or otherwise, does not quite dispose of the problem of "theoretical entities" in natural science. Here, where reference is ostensibly to the physical world, the use of terms for unobservables, neutrons, photons, mesons, quanta, etc., has divided opinion between realism and instrumentalism. The latter holds that these terms

are purely computational devices . . . whose sole function is to facilitate the prediction of observable facts. Contrariwise, the realistic interpretation asserts that at least some theoretical concepts refer to actually existing entities. . . . I do not think we need to resort to some obscure or questionable metaphysical speculations in order to resolve the issue of positivistic [instrumentalistic] versus realistic interpretation of scientific theories. It seems obvious to me that a well-confirmed theory, as for example the atomic theory, entitles us to ascribe existence (reality) to the atoms. After all, the sum of their masses makes up (at least approximately) the mass of a macro-object (such as a brick). Similarly, the total electric charge located on the surface of a large metal sphere is the sum of the charges of the individual electrons.[3]

Besides empirical confirmations, other considerations lend the weight of probability to the realistic view. The unobservables of natural science are intended to answer several different questions. Certainly they are intended to serve as predictive devices, as instrumentalists hold, and in this respect they are reducible to mathematical expressions, although the question lingers: expressions of what? But as a cognitive enterprise, theoretical natural science is faced with more questions than what will exist on the

[3] Herbert Feigl, "Philosophical Tangents of Science," *Current Issues in the Philosophy of Science* (New York: Holt, Rinehart & Winston, 1961), pp. 5-6. Cf. May Brodbeck, "Structure of Science," *Science*, vol. 134, Oct. 6, 1961, pp. 997-98.

observational surface of nature in the future. There is the question of what exists past, present, future, below and beyond the observational surface. Obviously, something does. And the more our instruments penetrate this surface, beginning with premicroscopic and pretelescopic days, the more we discover that something wonderfully real and potent appears to exist there. To discard this search is to abandon one of the most obvious and needed contributions that natural science might make to knowledge. I say needed, for inasmuch as there is evidently more than an observational surface to nature, some theory of what is below this surface is clearly required if the aim to bring systematic unity into our awareness of things is to do justice to this awareness as well as to grow beyond superficial understanding. There *is* something there. Also, natural science would seem to be in the best position to say what is there. Thirty or so basic theoretical entities [4] may not depict this subobservational region with completeness or accuracy. But they appear to be getting at something. Instrumentalism here seems to be a shortchanging of the cognitive aim for the superficial cash value of mathematical computation.

Terms for theoretical entities in natural science should not be confused with symbolic adjuncts used there and in symbolism generally. These adjuncts: "+," "−," "and," "but," "either," "or," and others, are not like "photon," "neutron," "electron"—symbols ostensibly employed for their objective reference. They are used primarily to organize other symbols into larger symbolic complexes. Sometimes called logical or "syncategorematical" [5] words, they symbolize or mean certain connections *in* the tissue of knowledge, not features of things outside of knowledge.

[4] Chen Ning Yang, *Elementary Particles: A Short History of Some Discoveries in Atomic Physics* (Princeton: Princeton University Press, 1962).
[5] Braithwaite, *Scientific Explanation*, p. 84.

A person may argue that in "The dog and the doll stand side by side" the word "and" symbolizes a conjunction of fact in the things known; and no doubt symbolic complexes often are constructed in ways that parallel the way things are in objective existence. But such parallelisms I think are superficial and not fundamental. The important point is not that each component of a symbolic complex corresponds to a discrete factual component of the object, but that the symbolic components unite to express a meaning that brings unity into our awareness of the diversity of the object. If a symbolic complex does this, it has performed its cognitive task. The one-to-one correspondence between the parts of the symbolic complex and the parts of the object is irrelevant, and often a chance affair. Indeed, had the sentence above been "The dog stands alongside the doll," the conjunction "and" in the symbolism would not have existed yet the physical conjunction of the dog and the doll would still have been expressed.

The appearance in the sciences of terms for theoretical entities occurs at an advanced level after much else has happened in the realm of meaning. Not only has primitive awareness and the continual storing of its experiences already had considerable play, but the artificialization of this awareness by the introduction of basic vocabularies has been well advanced. In their dictionary meanings, I have said, words have only a fraction of their full concrete meaning. Yet this dictionary meaning is of the highest importance for the advancement of knowledge. Words—nouns, pronouns, adjectives, verbs—denote recurrent objects. There is no point in introducing a word into a language if it is to be used once in all eternity. A word stabilizes cognition, affixing it to an object or kind of object that will occur again and again. It encourages cognition in the direction of universality. This is a necessary development if knowledge is to become adequate to the aim of encompassing things in their full sweep. To gain definiteness in this respect the knower must already have some background from primitive awareness, something from the past to connect with the present. A word draws together current and previous experience under a single rubric, and from this process slowly emerges our set of publicly serviceable concepts.[6]

Of course, this particular aspect of words is what most entails the loss of meaning I have mentioned. When words are used to emphasize the recurrent in experience, the rich transient meanings get stripped away, the bare bones of universality stick out. Immediacy is sacrificed to range. To this extent words are a very abstract and limited vehicle of knowledge, cutting away a vast penumbra of sensations, images, intuitions, feelings, to give us a stable and clear-cut public meaning. Yet language is capable of amplifying the cognitive power in numerous important directions. "We can store up our inferences for reconsideration, improve or reject them, build vast systems of them. . . . We have, through language, detached reasoning from its natural environment and given it the power of turning back on itself." [7] But perhaps the most fundamental way in which language amplifies our cognitive power is in connection with concept formation. It is therefore most important that we are clear about concepts and concept formation.

Concepts

Concepts are often described as word-meanings. This is not entirely accurate. A scientific formula, chemical, electrical, or other, may embody a concept, as "H_2O" embodies the chemical concept of water. Indeed any symbol providing material for thought as distinct from perception may embody a concept. Concepts are also described as meanings

[6] Cf. Vygotsky, *Thought and Language*, especially chap. 5.
[7] Marjorie Grene, *The Knower and the Known* (New York: Basic Books, 1966), p. 83.

of universal range. Perhaps most of them are. But concepts
are not limited to these. One may have a concept of Na-
poleon or Waterloo, of any individual human being or
historical situation. Such concepts involve a reference to,
and a description believed to be true of, the entity in question. Concepts of this sort restore some of the concreteness
lost in the abstract universal concept. They include our
concepts of our most intimate possessions and friends, and
extend to the widest fields of individual being, even to the
universe.

In our society, the explicit learning of concepts usually begins with an instructor correlating a word and
object by pointing and uttering the word. The concepts
thus absorbed are prefabricated meanings ready-made for
social communication. For various reasons connected with
the instructor or his social circle, many of these concepts
are poorly formed. When they are not re-examined in
terms of a proper principle, they lead to error or misunderstanding. Indeed, a cynic or philosopher might say
that all the key concepts of popular thought from freedom
and democracy on down need a critical overhauling. What
principle should govern such criticism to make concept
formation provide serviceable materials of knowledge?

This principle I think lies midway between the general
logical principle *A* is *A* and a specific network of rigid
categories such as Kant seems to have believed existed in
the human mind. The principle is a normative demand,
namely, that a concept referring to an object O shall contain all symbolic components necessary to give the awareness required in a situation of object O. Nothing necessary
shall be omitted, and no more included. I have called this
principle material necessity, and although a concept may
accumulate more components than the principle requires,
concepts that are serviceable in knowledge always conform

to its positive requirements up to the point they must do so in the situation in which they are functioning.

This principle obviously applies to concepts of constructed objects. An elegant construction in the abstract formal realm will assign to its terms just those properties necessary for the terms to perform their role in the construction, no more, or less. But perhaps the chief application of the principle is in the empirical realm. Here the principle suggests particularly that a concept may be conceived as a rule. Thus, the concept "iron" may be conceived as a rule which specifies all the symbolic components needed in a situation for a unified awareness of the substance iron. The rule says that X must be admitted, and also Y and Z, where X and Y and Z are necessary for awareness to grasp the object iron in the relevant context. This rule follows upon acceptance of material necessity as the principle of concept formation, and obviously it defines the empirical concept as it is when it is most serviceable in knowledge.

Besides this rule conception, the principle of material necessity explains such prominent characteristics of empirical concepts as their growth, plasticity, and demise. A kind of Darwinian version of the empirical concept has had a vogue in recent times. Darwin's "central conceptions are readily transposed to cognition, and have in recent times led to a theory of knowledge, in which concepts, like species, are regarded as plastic and variable, having a natural genesis and a capacity to survive according to the degree to which they fit the concrete situation to which they are applied." [8] One may hesitate to characterize concepts as mutations or chance variations, though the first appearance of some concepts seems as mysterious as mutations were to Darwin. But at least the growth, plasticity,

[8] Ralph Barton Perry, *Philosophy of the Recent Past* (New York: Charles Scribner's Sons, 1926), p. 27.

and survival of empirical concepts follow closely the Darwinian formula. These concepts change shape, expand and
contract, as material necessity requires, and they disappear
altogether, except as vestigial organs in popular lore, when
they are no longer able to meet this demand of the cognitive enterprise. In his description of metaphysical concepts as "fluid" and scientific concepts as "rigid," Bergson,
I believe, exaggerates the character of both types.[9] In science or metaphysics, when a concept "fits the situation" or
is adequate to descriptive needs, it is under no obligation
to change, and is exempt, at least momentarily, from the
perpetual flux. But because the demands of expanding investigations are being placed constantly on concepts in both
fields, even the most "fixed" concepts often must give way
to modifications or perish. Thus, the concepts of space and
time, mass and gravity, in physics, which in the eighteenth
century seemed established for all eternity, have yielded
to the relentless requirements of material necessity, and
have been considerably modified in recent times. If concepts are rules of coordination serving as means to ends,
if their function is to conform to an aim constantly extending into more remote and complex areas, the growth,
plasticity, and disappearance of even the most far-reaching
concepts would appear to be a perfectly natural consequence. To be open-ended or open-textured would seem to
be the normal condition of the empirical concept.

Besides these properties, material necessity explains
other important features of concepts such as the requirement
of simplicity. Since an empirical concept is a rule admitting
only what is necessary for the requisite awareness, that
concept doing its job adequately and admitting the few-
est components clearly is preferable, involving less fuss
yet full value. Ockham's Razor is an obvious corollary of

[9] Henri Bergson, *Introduction to Metaphysics*, trans. T. E. Hulme
(New York: G. P. Putnam's Sons, 1912), p. 65 ff.

material necessity. So is the subjective universality required of scientific concepts and theories. The cognitive requirement of concepts and theories in the natural sciences is that they be true not merely for the investigator who originates them, but also for all competent investigators of a problem. "Science is the study of those judgements concerning which universal agreement can be obtained." [10] The sciences try to formulate universally acceptable concepts and theories, and when, for example, a concept of metal fatigue or a theory of chemical combination is accepted, it is accepted as true not merely for the investigator who formulated it and for his laboratory, city, state, and nation, but for any investigator in any laboratory in any city, state, or nation, provided this investigator studies the metal or chemical combination under the general conditions in which the concept or theory is said to be true. This concept or theory is considered as necessary for any investigator, as for the original investigator, and, if it is found not to be so under the specified conditions, it is promptly questioned, and usually modified or rejected. The reign of necessity is as deep and extensive as genuine knowledge in any empirical field, though this is most conspicuously true in the natural sciences.

Potentialities

"A word is a microcosm of human consciousness." [11] In fact, any symbol is. Our first symbols, sensations, feelings, images, are our awareness in initial form. Our higher-order symbols, such as words correctly learned, enlarge and develop this awareness until it begins to reach to the most obscure corners of the universe. The radical behavioristic reduction of concepts to word-sounds and thoughts to subvocal thoracic disturbances would leave us with a world in which we did many things but were actually con-

[10] Campbell, *What Is Science?*, p. 27.
[11] Vygotsky, *Thought and Language*, p. 153.

scious of nothing. It would skim off all meaning and leave
only doing (the American Dream, some say, but hardly a
vision universally acceptable). The behaviorist is right,
however, in insisting upon a mooring for meaning, a material base such as a symbol provides. There may be
thoughts beyond words as there is knowledge before words,
but not thoughts beyond symbols. Symbols are the very
"stuff" of cognitive consciousness or the learned extensions
of this consciousness available to our awareness.

I have called symbols "materials," but in knowledge
they are arrayed in various forms. These forms are the
topic of the next chapter. The point to be noticed here is
merely the potentiality for complex order implicit in symbols as indigenous elements or grafted extensions of awareness. They can take on all the order that awareness in its
most subtle reaches can. This order is of two general types:
psychological order such as the sequences and associations
that form in our experience; and normative order such as
the logical, semantical, and syntactical orders that are generated in our sequential cognitions by the cognitive aim.
As elements of awareness our symbols are born servants of
the ongoing architectural processes of our experience, and
in cognition these processes, if required, do not hesitate to
use even the most intricate possibilities of psychological
and normative order when these can be serviceable in expanding the area of awareness.

The capacity for formal complexity, however, is not
the only potentiality of symbols. They also have expressive
possibilities. Symbols can express emotion, a cry may signify distress. They can express a personality even in a
phrase: "Someone drops a phrase and you say to yourself,
'No one else could have said just that thing in just that way.'
It is like a portrait of the man." [12] Above all, symbols can

[12] Margaret Bourke-White, *Portrait of Myself* (New York: Simon and
Schuster, 1963), p. 234.

illumine cognitively or express for awareness the being and nature of the universe and of the items of the universe of which we are a part. This cognitive expressiveness is perhaps the supreme potentiality of symbols in the domain of knowledge. From it all the uses of knowledge must directly flow. It is important to see, however, that this expressiveness would not be possible without the formal potentialities of symbols, and that its unities of meaning are conditioned by these formal possibilities.

V

Form

Psychological Order

Awareness involves consciousness of layout or configuration. It may be the layout of a scene before us, or of the kaleidoscopic sensations within us as we doze off to sleep. But everywhere awareness apprehends diversity in an arrangement of some sort, differentiated and connected, loosely or tightly. The system of relations pervading this diversity and constituting its organization is its shape, structure, or form.

Form exists not only in the field of which we are aware; it is equally present in awareness itself. In some cases, the arrangement of our symbols there seems to be a mere reflection of object order. But actually it is usually quite different. Two entities, of which we become aware, may coexist, a tree up the street and to our right, a tree down the street and to our left. But though the entities coexist, our awareness of them usually is sequential, now of one tree, now of the other. Sequential order is indeed the most elementary formal feature of the knowing process, which always occurs in time.

To some extent this sequential order is a result of our physiology. Our receptor, neural, and cerebral mechanisms,

70

like mechanisms generally, follow space-time laws. They act sequentially, and as used in cognition they induce a sequential pattern in our awareness. Generally, however, this order or pattern in our awareness is called psychological rather than physiological, and this is the term I shall employ. By psychological order I shall mean the sequential, historical order in which cognition occurs, and the connections that develop among its content from this historical order. It is the sequence of the knower's symbols, and the temporally determined associations and relations that grow within the sequential order of his symbols.

The intricacy of this historical network is sometimes astounding even in simplest cases. A person may first learn a word in temporal conjunction with another, "soft" and "Mama," and this sequential connection, fixed in memory, may subtly influence his reaction all of his life to things called "soft" and "Mama." From tiny associations such as this, extended in various ways, enlarging constantly, a great web of connections takes shape in the individual mind. Living in a particular environment, a Baconian Cave, he may form many such connections that are acutely provincial. Also, the depths in which these symbolic connections are stored are unstable. Relations shift about. Having experienced recurrent things in different sequences, changes in association inevitably occur. As a result, the psychological order is not only inclined to be provincial (a structure of symbols differing from group to group, even from person to person), it is also likely to be very unreliable, an arrangement of cognitive content as full of uncertainties as it is of surprise.

Nevertheless, a great deal of so-called thinking is based on this devious order. Much ordinary uncritical thinking is simply memory reproducing the sequential connections in which items were learned. The strength of these memory bonds often deeply shapes the tone of this thinking. A person who has learned strongly to connect "patriotism" with "pride" will respond to an appeal to his patriotism in a much different way, intellectually and emotionally, than will a person who has learned to connect "patriotism" with "hypocrisy." The "popular" mind is constantly being swayed by deftly manipulated psychological connections. So much of advertising, appealing to the popular mind, is dedicated to building the "right" sequential order in it. If an advertiser can connect the name of his product with some high-octane word, phrase, picture, or action, so that when a person sees or hears one he thinks of the other, he is commonly believed to have reached a peak achievement in his profession. Obviously, thinking in the psychological order has its treacheries. To trust it implicitly, as some people do, is to invite cognitive disaster.

Yet symbols arranged in the psychological order are of the greatest importance in the enterprise of knowledge. When we have learned the parts of a poem, a geometrical proof, a way of building a doghouse in a definite sequential order, and are called upon to say how the thing goes, we usually think of the poem, proof, or building routine in its learned psychological order. All cognition in which memory is a major factor is heavily dependent on this order. Indeed, it provides us with a great store of learning, and a person possessing a rich and wide-ranging memory has an exceptional potential for the advancement of learning. I say "potential" because the psychological order even at its best fails to qualify as a perfectly suitable cognitive type of symbolic form. It has several defects of which three seem most important.

First, the psychological order is ineradicably private. It arranges symbolic content autobiographically, in the way in which this content has occurred in the personal history of the knower. Some connections in one individual may be the same as in other individuals, even a large number may.

But a great many are likely to be different owing to each individual's diverse capacities and circumstances. The inter-subjective universality of knowledge is not notably characteristic of its structures. Second, the psychological order is a record of past sequences, and offers no guarantee that its connections will fit the future. Also, the stronger the psychological order, the deeper are its roots in the past, and the less flexibility it has to cope with the novel and the future. But perhaps the chief defect of the psychological order as a knowledge structure is its lack of a certifying cognitive principle. It gives us the settled order of symbols as these have occurred in the life of the individual. But to what extent this expresses the way things are or only the private apprehensions and misapprehensions of the knower, it does not disclose. We must go beyond the merely sequential order to determine this, and introduce some kind of normative principle.

Logical Order

The most elementary demand of normative order in knowledge is that the symbols we arrange be free of contradiction. Without this, whatever awareness we appear to gain through one symbol or set of symbols we destroy by the sequent contradicting symbol or set of symbols, and our total exertion comes to nought. This requirement of formal consistency is usually called logical, and the laws of logic (the laws of formal logic) are customarily described as the laws of formal consistency. Clearly, such laws formulate an essential of any symbolic complex that is to qualify as knowledge.

The requirement of formal consistency appears in our early awareness. Here we expect the variety of our symbols to settle into an apparently consistent unity or we are puzzled or confused by it. Such experience of consistency does not itself guarantee that our awareness is knowledge.

It is only the first requirement. In more advanced cases this is obviously so. A prosecutor may argue that a person is guilty of a crime, and draw all available knowledge of the circumstances into a consistent argument supporting an equally consistent conclusion. Yet this logically coherent structure of premises and conclusion may turn out to be false, and not knowledge at all.

Formal consistency, however, has long been universally recognized as one requirement of knowledge. Its possibilities of systematic use have been extensively explored, and a sizable variety of formal systems embodying purely logical order has been produced. Ordinarily, in such systems the denotation of the terms is unspecified, and the investigation focuses on the way the terms may be consistently combined within the stipulations that the system lays down. Arithmetic, geometry, even mathematics as a whole, as I have said, are sometimes described in this way. The heart of such systems is the set of postulates (axioms equal postulates) stipulating what is formally permissible in the system. The terms, as I say, are undefined, except for the properties assigned to them in the postulates. The system is articulated by a series of theorems about the relations of the terms and a series of proofs that establish that the theorems are the consistent consequences of the postulates.[1] Such formal systems display the great variety of consistent arrangements in which anything can be arrayed which can be substituted for the terms of the system.

In a sense, these symbolic edifices are elaborate tautologies. But they do show explicitly what *is* in the premises, and usually this was not known beforehand. We may say therefore that while obedience to the rules of formal logic does not certify that a symbolic structure is knowledge, the development of formal systems embodying

[1] Alfred North Whitehead, *Science and the Modern World* (New York: Macmillan Co., 1939, chap. 2; *idem, An Introduction to Mathematics* (New York: Henry Holt & Co., 1911).

these rules does provide us with a certain kind of knowledge. Indeed, these systems make two major additions to our cognitive possessions. First, they show us the many possibilities of the principles of formal consistency, the many types of systems they can produce. Second, they can become powerful instruments for the articulation of other knowledge wherever items in a subject matter exhibit properties approximating or coinciding with the properties of the terms of the formal system. Once you are able to identify exactly or approximately entities in a nonformal system with the terms of a formal system (e.g., entities in physical nature with terms in geometry), the theorems of the formal system apply to the nonformal system, and the formal system provides an awareness not only of abstract formal possibility but of actual world order.

This latter knowledge has often been supplied by well-wrought formal systems in modern times.

Investigations of the structure of fundamental particles have demonstrated, more convincingly than before, that the theory of group representations is a powerful tool in the study of quantum systems. . . . The present state of research in theoretical physics indicates that some modern algebraic theories—noncompact groups, general associative algebras, and so on—that until recently were thought to be too abstract to be useful in physics will play an essential role in the developments of the near future. It is remarkable that since the beginning of theoretical physics every major new step had its own distinct mathematical discipline from which it is inseparable, as though each new level of natural philosophy requires a new language. From the infinitesimal calculus and ordinary differential equations in Newtonian mechanics, to partial differential equations in Maxwellian field theory, to linear algebra and operators in Hilbert space in the quantum mechanics of Heisenberg and Dirac, to the theory of functions of complex variables in S-matrix theory, the mathematics has been not merely a tool but fundamentally interwoven with the physical concepts.[2]

[2] A. O. Barut, "Quantum Theory and Mathematics," *Science*, vol. 155, no. 3763, Feb. 10, 1967, p. 683.

The conclusion of this section, however, must be that logical order is a necessary but not a sufficient principle in knowledge. Consistency, conformity to formal logic, does make a symbolic array valid formally. But the question remains whether the symbolic array is valid objectively or of its object. To determine this, something more than abstract logical order is required.

Semantical Order

In reverie, recollection, meditation, and dreams each of us finds a wealth of symbolic content arrayed in sequential order. Some of it makes sense, as we say. Some does not. What is the difference? Sometimes it is the presence or absence of logical order. Incoherence and contradiction infect many of these episodes. But this is not always the case. Indeed, some of these symbolic structures are fantastically coherent, almost like mathematical conclusions deduced from mathematical premises. Yet we do not hesitate to describe them as nonsense. When pressed, we may say, they are out of touch with "reality". They do not describe any state of affairs that we believe to be actual or really possible in known circumstances.

By semantical order I mean the order in a symbolic array sufficient for description of an object or state of affairs by the array. Sequences of symbols in all areas, in conversation and news reports, no less than in science and philosophy, enter the semantical arena whenever they claim to describe some state of affairs, inner or outer, actual or possible, and to make sense in regard to this object matter. What is the criterion for testing such claims? What is the principle of semantical order? My suggestion is that a symbolic structure has semantical order when its content is arranged so as to provide the object awareness that the cognitive aim in the situation requires. A structure with such an order of content would deliver as it claimed the sense of the situation, the meaning needed in the context, and this is what we must ask of symbolic arrays that are semantically acceptable.

An illustration may help to elucidate this point. A person says: "I'd like to know where I can find a calendar," and another replies: "There is a calendar on that table," as there is. The second statement, as an arrangement of words giving what was needed for the awareness required by the cognitive aim in the situation, would be said, in the present sense, to have semantical order. Obviously, this order is tied in with the content of knowledge. Indeed, it is the supremely necessary order of just such content. I shall therefore consider it further in the discussion of content in the next chapter.

Semantical order as here described is clearly different from psychological order. Symbols may be arranged in various psychological patterns, yet, as I have said, make no sense at all, e.g. "dateless calendar." Also, semantical order is different from mere logical or formal order. A sequence of symbols, such as "There is a calendar on the bed," may be perfectly coherent, yet not meet at all the cognitive requirement of the above situation, there being no calendar on the bed. Finally, semantical order is different from the physical order with which it can be and has sometimes been confused. Spinoza's famous theorem that the order and connection of ideas is the same as the order and connection of things [3] is an invitation to confuse the semantical with the physical order. Kant's view that the categories of knowledge are the forms of nature breeds a similar confusion. Each order has a fundamentally different material, symbols versus physical things, which naturally require different methods of handling, and different types of control.

The confusion of these two orders, the semantical and the physical, is sometimes aided by language. We speak of

[3] Spinoza, *Ethics*, Part II, Proposition VII.

a law of nature as a statement describing a pattern of events in nature, e.g. Newton's first law. But, as I have mentioned, we also speak of the law of nature as a pattern or constant conjunction in nature itself. In the one case, the law is a symbolic structure, and as referring to an objective conjunction, is subject to the principle of semantical order. In the other case, the law is a constituent of nature itself. This confusion becomes distressingly acute in our language about law in the human realm. Here moral and civil laws are ordinarily considered to be statements prescribing the behavior of human beings, e.g. the Ten Commandments. Yet we also speak of law as if it were an external ontological thing and we even speak of the moral order of the universe.

Syntactical Order

Syntax in the strict sense is that part of grammar dealing with sentences and sentence construction in such ordinary languages as English, French, German, Russian.[4] In one obvious sense syntactical order differs from semantical order as just described. Semantical order applies to all symbolic arrays, lingual, prelingual, alingual, while syntactical order applies to one limited type. But there is a much more important difference. In English "The square root of two is a Russian peasant" has a perfectly correct syntactical structure. It has a subject, copula, predicate, and is arranged according to the rules of English grammar. Yet semantically it is nonsense. It has no descriptive application, and seems unlikely ever to have one, at least as its terms now are ordinarily understood.[5]

What role in knowledge has syntactical order in the narrow or strict sense? Clearly, it has some. A vast amount of current and traditional knowledge is carried in ordinary

[4] Noam Chomsky, *Syntactic Structures* (The Hague: Mouton & Co., 1965), p. 11.
[5] Cf. Chomsky, *Syntactic Structures,* chap. 9.

language, and were words jumbled every which way in its use, this language would not succeed in conveying this knowledge. It seems too strong to say, however, that, in the cognitive use of ordinary language, proper syntactical order, like logical and semantical order, is a *sine qua non* of knowledge. A person may speak and even write ungrammatically, yet convey fully and successfully what he knows of a situation. Of course he may also convey no knowledge at all. Perhaps the most precise way to phrase the matter is to say that the syntax of a language comprises the rules traditionally followed and/or currently accepted for the construction of those sentences which express or transmit meanings most reliably in that language. In other words, syntactical order is a highly desirable and even sometimes, but not always, an obligatory order in a certain type of cognitive structure. In this respect, it differs from both logical and semantical order not only in nature and breadth, but also in its role in cognition, since logical order and semantical order are obligatory in symbolic structures that would qualify as knowledge.

Syntax may be construed in a broader sense than as the rules for sentences and sentence construction in ordinary languages. Symbolic arrays that have subparts which are analogous in some degree to words and combine into larger units, like sentences conveying a unity of meaning, may be said to have syntax: mathematics, music, sign language, pantomime, dance, the communication systems of insects and animals, the prelingual systems imposed by human beings on apes and other creatures, and more. This extension of the concept of syntax raises in larger and more suitable form some questions about language to be considered in the next section. Here our central interest is in the role of syntax, in its broad (and limited) senses, in knowledge. This role I think is to constitute that arrangement of unit symbols which is thought to facilitate the most reliable expression and diffusion of meaning in the symbolism. The arrangement may be a generally accepted set of rules of combination such as the syntax of the English language. Or it may be a new set of rules invented to make what is being conveyed in a new symbolism more intelligible: the syntax of a new world language, or, insofar as they make a cognitive claim, the syntax of a new style of dance or music. In either case, the concern is not with the logical nor with the objective correctness of the expressions but with ways of forming these expressions so that they will be most intelligible as parts of the symbolism. This effort to be serviceable embodied in syntactical order clearly may remove a major block to expressing or transmitting one's understanding of a situation. An intelligible symbolism, logically and syntactically well-ordered, and yielding the required awareness of the object of cognition, is probably the simplest comprehensive definition of objective knowledge.

Ordinary language where syntactical order reigns has been a prominent topic in recent philosophy, and some questions about it, especially about its logical and semantical quality, now call for discussion.

Ordinary Language

Ordinary language can have many functions. It can admonish, direct, deride, incite, perform ritual, and much more. But it is with ordinary language in its cognitive function that we are here concerned. Its most obvious characteristic in this respect would seem to be its limitations. So much of our knowledge is prelingual or alingual, embodied in natural symbols such as sensations or in artificial nonordinary-language symbols, such as mathematics, that a most modest claim for the role of ordinary language in knowledge would seem to be called for. Moreover, as the product of folkways and everyday usage, ordinary language is, as Bacon said, infested with idols. It is a medium for provincial clichés, prejudices, and confusions. It is also poorly prepared to digest novel and refined insights, requiring interminable additions for this purpose, including the ever-expanding special vocabularies of natural science and technology. There is also the Whorfian thesis of linguistic relativity. The "structure of a human being's language influences the manner in which he understands reality,"[6] and different ordinary languages, English and Hopi for example, make different "segmentations of experience." [7] As a consequence, the knowledge conveyed in any ordinary language is always partial and one-sided, and at its best relative to the limiting linguistic forms of the language of the knower.[8]

These logical and semantical shortcomings, even excluding the Whorfian thesis, (it remains controversial),[9] make one hesitate to accept a philosophy advocating that in the standard use of an ordinary language, such as English, the solution of all philosophical problems can be found. No doubt a number of minor philosophical puzzles in Anglo-American philosophy can be eliminated by a more clear and consistent use of standard English, and efforts in this direction should be praised and encouraged. But the result of giving ultimate authority in any broad field of knowledge to any ordinary language is to freeze the prejudices and practices of the limited agencies that so far have been the creators of the language, and to disregard the basic concept of language as an instrument to be shaped in

[6] Benjamin Lee Whorf, *Language, Thought, and Reality*, ed. John B. Carroll (Cambridge, Mass.: M.I.T. Press, 1956), p. 23.

[7] Whorf, *Language*, p. 26.

[8] Hanson, *Patterns of Discovery*, p. 26: "Our visual sensations may be 'set' by language forms; how else could they be appreciated in terms of what we know?"

[9] Whorf, *Language*, pp. 27-30.

any novel direction that the ends of human domains such as knowledge require.[10]

Perhaps the flexibility and nontribalism required of an ordinary language to cope with the constant growth of knowledge can be suitably provided by conceiving such language as a game, as some language philosophers do. Using language would be like playing chess or poker—manipulating artificial counters according to generally accepted rules which might be changed as need arises. In some respects certainly this is a useful idea, emphasizing the artificial and conventional aspects of language. But it is not very adequate to the full character of language. When I fill in a crossword puzzle, I might be said to be using language in a gamelike way. But ordinarily, using language is not a pastime but part of the serious side of living and thinking. To be sure, besides involving conventional rules, using language has other gamelike features, such as the exercise of cunning and craft to exploit its various possibilities. But the crucial question still concerns the purpose of language: recreation, pastime, to fill leisure intriguingly—the original and distinctive purpose of a game, or to serve living and thinking in major efforts. In the world in which we live and are likely to live, I think there can be little doubt about the appropriate answer.

[10] Gilbert Ryle contends that philosophers have been victims of the pitfalls of ordinary language with its alleged systematically misleading expressions. See Gilbert Ryle, "Ordinary Language," *Philosophy and Ordinary Language,* ed. C. E. Caton (Urbana: University of Illinois Press, 1963), and *idem* "Systematically Misleading Expressions," *Logic and Language,* ed. A. Flew, first series (Oxford: Blackwell & Co., 1951). Blanshard has shown very convincingly that the most common and urgent problems of philosophy, including those in the theory of knowledge, are not products of linguistic confusion at all, and are not solved by reference to standard English or a perfect dictionary. See Brand Blanshard, *Reason and Analysis* (LaSalle, Ill.: Open Court Publishing Co., 1962), pp. 347-81. Cf. Alfred North Whitehead, *Modes of Thought* (New York: G. P. Putnam's Sons, 1958), p. 235, "The Fallacy of the Perfect Dictionary."

Despite its shortcomings, an ordinary language, well codified, used coherently and responsively, extended carefully by select additions of other artificial symbols such as symbols from mathematics, can make very significant contributions to knowledge. One such contribution I think is stability. Such a language permits us to embody great segments of knowledge in established and accessible symbolic structures that can preserve and transmit these accumulations. More elementary and far-reaching perhaps is another contribution: even when its words are learned by association with surface stimuli,[11] a language involves the reconstruction of native cognition in the direction of universality. By learning an ordinary language with its many terms for recurrent properties and events and things, we slowly grasp the meaning of general terms, and at an early age [12] we begin to form general ideas or general concepts. Such concepts are indispensable to the higher reaches of knowledge. From the beginning the root aim of knowledge is comprehensive awareness, wholeness of view. To be able to string the vast diversity of properties and events and things on simple inclusive threads of clear-cut symbols is a tremendous advantage in this enterprise, and it is this that the formation of general concepts or at least of word-meanings of great generality enables us for the first time to do.

[11] Quine, *Word and Object,* chaps. 1 and 2.
[12] Vygotsky, in *Thought and Language,* believes it is about the age of puberty. See chap. 5.

VI

Content

Its Nature

Symbolic arrays not only have form, they symbolize. They stand for or mean various things. This is their content. This content may have various uses. It may be used to express an emotion. Deryck Cooke has argued that through long conditioning but also from intrinsic form, figures and patterns of preserial Western music express very definite emotions and that composers have recognized this by repeatedly calling on these figures and patterns when they wished to express these emotions.[1] In practical everyday contexts, symbolic arrays may be employed to indicate an action to be performed, a wish to be denied, a hope to be fulfilled. Indeed, as gesture and language, they may be woven into the texture of any kind of human activity and their content serve the needs of any of the operations being performed there.

What is important for our present purpose, however, are symbolic arrays in their cognitive use. Perhaps no symbolic array except sheer nonsense is without some actual or potential cognitive use, and even sheer nonsense can il-

[1] Deryck Cooke, *The Language of Music* (London: Oxford University Press, 1959, 1960; Oxford Paperback no. 44, 1962).

84

lustrate the meaning of sheer nonsense. Artistic structures, even the most romantically expressive, often give very moving insights into the nature of an emotion or emotional sequence, and so provide knowledge. What determines them as artistic rather than cognitive is not their emotive or other content, but the purpose they are serving. Primarily, they are serving and/or designed to serve an aesthetic rather than a noetic purpose, and in this context they are taken as artistic, although their noetic aspect may function throughout.

At their best, symbolic structures used for cognitive purposes are commonly said to be true or the truth. Before discussing this advanced stage of cognitive content, certain more elementary circumstances affecting this content should be recalled.

Human cognition occurs within numerous limiting conditions. There is the temperament of the knower, the peculiar individual history of his learning processes, and the value background he has acquired, all of which influence the cognitive selections and decisions he will make or wish to emphasize. There is the inescapable temporality of the knowing process: "No significant and useful idea can be rendered entirely transparent at an instant." [2] Insofar as the individual's knowledge is imbedded in language, there are the limiting conditions of his language: "Every language will inevitably contain expressions whose adequate understanding requires a consideration of the activities of those who use the language as much as it involves a reference to the ostensible subject matter of that language." [3] There are also the many presuppositions of the knowing process, beginning with the laws of logic, which cannot be

[2] W. Donald Oliver, *Theory of Order* (Yellow Springs, Ohio: Antioch Press, 1951), p. 319.
[3] Ernest Nagel, "Operational Analysis as an Instrument for the Critique of Linguistic Signs," *Journal of Philosophy*, vol. 39, no. 7, March 26, 1942, p. 189.

rationally rejected without using them and assuming their correctness. Regarding the presuppositions of verification, Brightman writes: "Unless we presuppose the unity of the verifying self, the presence of data within self-experience, the purpose of verification, the validity of reason, the trustworthiness of memory (when tested by reason), the reality of time, and the reality of an objective world which is there when not observed or verified, no verification can occur."[4]

In short, a great complex of limiting factors converges in the formation of any cognitive structure. Human knowing is a human activity, and human knowledge is a human product; we must expect it to be deeply impregnated with human traits, especially the all-too-human limiting traits of human character and circumstance. And just as the full nature of a symbolic array is not clear unless the individual situation in which the array is being used, and the use of it in the situation, are clear, so the individual knower must be considered in all his assumptions and limitations for a full understanding of what he offers us as knowledge. But when all is said and done, it remains true that the symbolic structures offered by an individual as knowledge do claim to be reports of what is the case in the area of their objective reference. Moreover, when these structures are linguistic and the language is a shareable symbolism, such as an ordinary language or mathematics, these structures are commonly set forth and should be set forth as reports that all others who know the language and the situation would make or agree upon. The structures claim intersubjective universality as well as objectivity. In summary, cognitive structures may be colored by personal, social, intellectual, and any number of other limiting conditions. But they also have objective and universal aspects, and it is here that their truth or cognitive virtue, if any, is to be sought and estimated.

[4] E. S. Brightman, *A Philosophy of Religion* (Englewood Cliffs, N.J.: Prentice-Hall, 1947), p. 121.

I do not mean by this that knowledge and truth depend on a "public mind," even when this term means not an ontological ghost but your mind and others sharing a common meaning. You may be the first to know the truth of a situation. Your mind would then possess knowledge and truth without yet having shared with others this meaning of the situation. Intersubjective universality is an outstanding potential of knowledge and truth, necessary of actualization for their general acceptance. But it is not their epitome. Nor do I mean here that truth is limited even in linguistic contexts to what Quine has called "eternal sentences,"[5] sentences stripped of their space-time particularity. A sentence such as "There is copper oxide here-now" may be as true as any sentence that omits a space-time reference, such as "Copper oxide is green." The point is rather that the content of cognitive structures is more than their expression of the physical, personal, intellectual, social, and other limiting circumstances of the knower. These structures emerge as cognitive from their limiting human matrix, with content making a definite additional claim or the pretense of such a claim. And it is this that makes them candidates for truth and knowledge.

Truth

Truth, however, has many meanings. Literary critics speak of artistic and poetic truth. Sometimes they mean by this merely sincerity on the part of the novelist or poet. But often they mean that while the symbolic structures that the novelist or poet has created may not describe any actuality, they do describe what would be actual in the human or physical realm under the circumstances assumed and depicted. Philosophers contrast true (authentic) being and false (unauthentic) being. Plato meant by true being "what lasts, the eternal." Heidegger means by true (au-

[5] Quine, *Word and Object*, p. 12. See the section on eternity below.

thentic) being "full being, or being that is fully in possession of its phenomenological structure." In common
parlance, "true" usually means "honest," as when people describe a man who is telling the truth as honest. "True" also
means in common speech "what is straight and not
crooked," as when a person says that a wall or a human
character is built straight and true. No doubt there are more
meanings of true and truth,[6] but like most of those just
mentioned they are not our chief concern. Our subject is
cognitive truth, and our question is: When a symbolic structure is said to be knowledge or to be cognitively true or the
truth, what is meant by "true" and "the truth"? Only in this
sense, and insofar as the above meanings of truth are identi-
cal with this sense, shall we be concerned with truth in this
discussion.

Even limiting the subject in this way, it remains complex, since the theories of cognitive truth are numerous and
sometimes complicated. At the present time, they include
the coherence, correspondence, semantic, and pragmatic
theories of truth as outstanding examples. The procedure I
plan to follow is to state the theory of cognitive truth
emerging from our whole argument, elucidate it by some
comparisons with the other theories of truth just mentioned, then illustrate it further by a discussion of two
major types of truth—formal and material.

I summarize the theory as follows: A symbolic structure, lingual or alingual, is a configuration of symbols, cognitive materials in a form. When this structure is used in a
cognitive situation and supplies, or can supply, the awareness required by the cognitive aim in that situation, the
structure is true, a truth, or the truth. The power of a symbolic structure to function in this way is dependent on two

[6] See Alfred Hofstadter, "Truth of Being," *Journal of Philosophy*,
vol. 62, no. 7, April 1, 1965, pp. 167-73, for a review of various
meanings of truth.

factors. There are two criteria of truth. First, the structure must be a well-formed form, internally coherent, free of inner contradiction. Otherwise, it would cancel internally any awareness of its object that it aroused. Second, the structure must conform to the principle of material necessity. That is, a symbolic structure referring to object O shall contain all symbolic components necessary in the situation for the awareness, required by the cognitive aim, of object O. Nothing necessary shall be omitted, and no more need be included. This double-pronged theory of truth is clearly an emergent from our whole argument up to this point.

I will turn now to the other theories of truth above mentioned. First, the coherence theory. A symbolic structure may be coherent, free of inner contradiction, yet it may not be true. Fantasies are often that way. So are descriptions of imaginary illnesses. To a doctor investigating such a nonexistent illness its internally coherent description would contain nothing he found in the allegedly afflicted person. Or, in our terms, the description would fail to provide the object-awareness required in the situation by the doctor's cognitive aim. Besides freedom from internal contradiction, however, coherence may have a second meaning. According to this, a symbolic structure is true if it brings coherence into our understanding of a cognitive situation. Or, to the degree that it does this, the symbolic structure is true. This theory coincides with our own if by "understanding" is meant the object-awareness required in a situation by the cognitive aim. Coherence is required of this object-awareness, and only to the degree that it is achieved does the awareness satisfy our first criterion of truth.

The correspondence theory usually ascribed to Spinoza and the early Wittgenstein is that there is a one-to-one parallelism between the parts of a symbolic array (Spinoza's ideas) and the parts of its object (Spinoza's things). Such a theory has defects already alluded to. In a cognitive situation, to be sure, there is a symbolic structure and an objective ensemble, and there may even be a part-to-part parallelism between the two. But there may not be. In a complex situation, a symbol or two may tell you truly all you want to know at the time about the situation, e.g., a sign reading "Battlefield Ahead." In a simple situation, as when one is explaining accurately a familiar object to a child, dozens of symbols including words and gestures may be required. Thus, a part-to-part parallelism may be non-existent in situations where the truth of the symbolism is known. Like coherence, however, correspondence may have another more acceptable interpretation. According to this, a symbolic structure is true if in a situation it corresponds in meaning—not necessarily in its symbol parts—to its object as known. Assuming that "its object as known" means an object of an awareness satisfying a cognitive aim, this statement of the correspondence theory I believe is merely a different version of our own theory with the coherence requirement unemphasized.

The semantic theory of truth is briefly that "The pavement is wet" is true if, and only if, the pavement is wet.[7] This theory itself seems true enough, so far as it goes. What it lacks is an indication of the cognitive setting in which truth occurs and the criteria that in this setting test the truth of an assertion. Our own theory might be described as the semantic theory with its omitted elements included. In any case, the semantic theory, as paraphrased above, leaves the context and the criteria that give specific being —flesh and blood—to truth indeterminate and undecided.

In broadest terms, the pragmatic theory is that a symbolic structure is true if it satisfies the human needs in the situation in which it is used. In this loose Jamesian form,

[7] A. Tarski, "The Semantic Theory of Truth," *Semantics*, ed. L. Linsky (Urbana: University of Illinois Press, 1952).

the theory confuses cognitive truth with general usefulness. Cognitive truth may have general usefulness, but to have this it must first be cognitively true. The pragmatic theory democratizes human needs, placing all on the same level. In giving context and life and vigor to the cognitive enterprise, emphasizing the role of striving and of a concrete setting, pragmatism has certainly made an important contribution. But its conception of truth, at least as formulated by James, seems too general to yield the specific and distinctive characteristics of cognitive truth. Moreover, even if the theory were formulated in cognitive terms, it would have to spell out these terms. To describe them, as Dewey does, as the consequences that follow from a symbolic structure is again too broad. These structures may have numerous types of consequences: economic, political, aesthetic, emotional, etc. Our theory would agree with pragmatism if the terms were described as a structure's cognitive consequences, and these consequences were described as a coherent object-awareness satisfying the cognitive aim in a situation under scrutiny.[8]

I think it is evident from the preceding discussion that while the adjective "true" is not illegitimate, it can, as Ramsey and Strawson argue, following Frege, be dispensed with.[9] A symbolic array that is true is a truth, and its statement as a truth can always be substituted for the statement that it is true.

It may be objected to our general account, however, that it imputes a certain undesirable subjectivity and relativity to the nature of truth. The cognitive aim of a given particular person, a pre-Copernican epicyclist for example,

[8] C. S. Peirce described these consequences as the sensible effects implied by an idea or theory. This seems at least to put the consequences in the cognitive sphere. For a statement and criticism of Peirce's views, see Blanshard, *Reason and Analysis,* pp. 192-97.

[9] G. Pitcher, ed., *Truth,* Contemporary Perspectives in Philosophy series (Englewood Cliffs, N.J.: Prentice-Hall, 1964), pp. 32-54.

may appear to be completely satisfied in his situation. Therefore, according to our account, he has achieved truth. Yet the person may not have the truth at all. This objection I think can be answered by recalling our description of the cognitive aim. In any situation, such as an investigation of planetary motion in our solar system, the cognitive aim is to achieve awareness of what is the case. An epicyclist may think he has achieved this, but investigation of his claim may show he did not. In our view, the cognitive goal is not personal satisfaction but object-awareness, and only if this occurs is this goal attained.

So much then for a statement of our theory of truth and some comparisons of it with other theories. I proceed now to illustrate and elucidate it further by a discussion of formal and material truth.

Formal Truth

A symbolic system is sometimes said to have formal truth if it is a consistent whole, such as an elementary tautological system. A system of this type certainly has a *sine qua non* of a true cognitive structure, and is true in a sense already mentioned, according to which a thing well-built or built on a coherent plan is said to be true, "straight and true." But this is not the sense in which I am using the term "truth" and shall use the term "formal truth." Such a well-built system, if internally consistent, I shall describe as formally valid or abstractly correct. It has formal validity or correctness rather than truth or formal truth.

Yet such formally correct systems may rightly be said to have truth in our sense, and formal truth. This occurs when they are viewed as saying something, as they do, about formal relations. As we have seen, geometries, according to some theorists, are composed of terms whose properties are fixed by the postulates of the system. The postulates stipulate the relations between the term per-

missible in the system, and the theorems state the additional
relations that are considered provable for the terms on the
basis of the postulates. Thus, what such a system says is
that if any thing has the initial relational properties assigned to the terms of the system, it will have the following additional relational properties stated in the theorems.
Or, if any things have the formal connections initially assigned to the terms, they will have the additional formal
connections established by the proofs. The system is a set
of assertions about formal relations, and as true of these, it
has truth in our sense, and formal truth.

Mathematics has been called an incomplete language,[10]
and in a certain respect, all purely formal systems are incomplete symbolic structures. They state what formal relations will exist where entities with properties matching the
initial properties of their terms actually exist. But they do
not state where these matching entities are, or even that
they exist. In other words, they do not tell us all that we
need to know for us to know that the theorems of the systems are true of actual existing things. Of these things
their truth is incomplete and hypothetical. They say: *if*
these things have such-and-such properties, they will have
the following additional properties. In this sense, so far
as ordinary existence goes, purely formal systems are incomplete symbolic structures.

I should add that systems having this kind of hypothetical formal truth are not limited to possible descriptions
of entities and relations in physical situations. Norms,
oughts, standards in human situations can be similarly
formalized, as in deontic logic.[11] Such systems do not say
that such-and-such norms, oughts, standards exist or rightly

[10] Boulding, *The Image*, p. 137 ff.
[11] Cf. Georg H. von Wright, *Norm and Action: A Logical Enquiry*
(New York: Humanities Press, 1963); *idem, The Varieties of Good-
ness* (New York: Humanities Press, 1943); and *idem,* "Deontic
Logic," *Mind,* 1951.

exist, but, if such norms, oughts, standards exist, the following actions are implied by them. In fact, deontic logic no more solves the problems of ethics than pure mathematics solves the problems of physics. But, if successful, it does provide a powerful insight to the ethicist, as pure geometry has provided a similar insight to the physicist. In this respect it has truth, but hypothetical truth. It can also be said to have formal truth, viewed as portraying the formal connections of norms, oughts, standards with actions.

Material Truth

Symbolic structures referring to things at hand ("This metal is iron," "This wall is solid") are often cited as simple examples of truth. In making clear a characteristic of these particulars (this metal, this wall) to anyone who understands the English language and examines the particulars, these statements would be true in our sense. To be sure, if examining the particulars led a person to say: "This metal is lead" or "This wall is hollow," the case would be different. But if the statements did give an examiner who understood the English meanings of "iron" and "solid" and the other terms an awareness of what was the case, they would have all of the qualities of true statements.

Simple illustrations such as these particular material statements can be misleading, however, if they are taken as the whole story about material truths. Beyond them are the numerous empirical generalizations and general concepts and theories of the sciences which are singularly different yet appear equally to claim material truth. These general structures have much more complex properties than the simple statements of ordinary daily life, and raise problems that the simple statements obscure or fail to raise in full form.

Before considering some of these in the next section, a few comments about particular empirical statements should be made. Some say that a sentence such as "This metal is iron" has an infinite number of implications. It implies that if you touch the object referred to under certain circumstances it will feel a certain way; if you mix it with sulphuric acid under certain conditions it will act a certain way, ad infinitum. Hence, unless you can complete an infinite number of investigations, which you cannot, you can never be sure that a statement such as "This metal is iron" is true or false. Let me note first of all that this argument is not a challenge to our theory of truth but to whether a certain type of material statement can be established as an illustration of this theory. But more directly, this argument that no material statement of the type cited can be established seems to labor under a misunderstanding of what is involved. Presumably a person who found the statement "This metal is iron" to be true would already know, for the purpose at hand, what a metal is and what differentiates iron as a metal. This background, not an infinite number of verifications, would be sufficient to enable him to find the statement to be true (or false). No further operation, such as tracing out an infinite number of consequences, would be required.

It may be that certain types of language are more suitable than others as mediums of truth. Wheelwright distinguishes between steno-language (rigid) and tensive language (flexible) and argues that only a flexible language is competent to convey the full sinuosity of What Is.[12] Perhaps it is artificial to divide languages into such types. But flexibility of language, as I have said, is necessary for the formation of adequate concepts, and it would appear to be equally necessary for the formulation of truths linguistically. Language must respond to our awareness, for

[12] Philip Wheelwright, *Metaphor and Reality* (Bloomington: Indiana University Press, 1962); *idem, The Burning Fountain* (Bloomington: Indiana University Press, 1954).

it is this awareness with its great flexibility, ranging from the meagerest sensation to the most comprehensive thought, that is the proper architect of knowledge. Appropriately, "A thought may be compared to a cloud shedding a shower of words," [13] and the words should take on the contour of the thought which is the active promulgator of a linguistic expression of cognitive stature.

Probably I should emphasize again that particular material statements, like cognitive expressions generally, occur ordinarily within a background of knowledge and opinion and often involve considerable sophistication about the surrounding world. In everyday situations. however, this background serves as an instrument to illumine quickly, by recognition or rapid analysis, the object under quizzical scrutiny, and where it is effective, it amplifies current awareness adequately. Indeed, in everyday contexts, learning would be of little value, knowledge of tradition and history of little use, if they did not form such an illuminating background. And this is ordinarily the posture of general ideas in ordinary situations, namely, as a background utility.

In Science

I have said that simple illustrations of particular material truths can be misleading, if taken as the whole story about material truth. In different contexts these truths have different standing. In everyday situations, they are usually the focus of attention to which our accumulations of ideas and experience are subservient. In the advanced sciences, however, these truths are frequently instruments for the building of conceptual schemes which are the chief focus of interest and the goal there of the cognitive enterprise. To be sure, a conceptual scheme in a science may direct attention to new material circumstances, and lead to new particular truths. It may be an instrument of discovery. There is a

[13] Vygotsky, *Thought and Language,* p. 150.

reciprocity between theory and observation, hypothesis and verification, even between theory and theory, and observation and observation, and in a complete account all of these factors would probably be pictured as means and ends.[14] Still, the great cognitive achievement of an advanced science usually is considered to be its basic conceptual scheme, and the cognitive ideal of such a science is often said to be to erect a conceptual scheme from which all lower-level hypotheses and all germane particular material statements regarding the inhabitants of its field can be deduced.[15]

There is a paradox here worth exploring a moment for the light it sheds on the cognitive enterprise. The ideal material truth, one would think, is one as close as possible to the object being investigated, and particular material truths would seem to come nearest to this ideal. Yet actually in those sciences where the quest for material truth has reached its highest and best-developed form, the ideal sought is a conceptual scheme that seems abstract and remote from actual objects, reaching them only indirectly and discursively by an elaborate deductive process. The solution of this paradox, I think, lies in recalling the cognitive aim in its ideal form. This aim is wholeness of view, the comprehensive outlook. In its fullest orbit, it is a seeking to know all that there is to know. An efficient conceptual scheme that spread-eagles the field, and is able to include under it as deductions the particular material truths of the field, is clearly a far superior fulfillment of this aim than any particular material statement or group of statements of limited range.

It may be objected that in the advanced natural sciences the symbolic structures offered to provide this high

[14] Cf. F. L. Will, "The Justification of Theories," *Philosophical Review*, vol. 64, no. 3, July, 1955, pp. 370-88.
[15] Cf. Braithwaite, *Scientific Explanation*, pp. 342-43, 351-52.

awareness are hypothetical and probable only. They give us only "iffy" perspectives, and conclusions so general and far-reaching that only omniscience could verify them as apodeictic. Also, several competing conceptual schemes sometimes are equally competent to unify and form a deductive base for the certified material statements about the field. But all of this can be freely admitted with no damage to the position above taken. In their conceptual schemes, the advanced natural sciences can be viewed simply as steps on the way, efforts—among the best we can make— to meet the demands of the cognitive venture. The cognitive aim in its broadest form sets up an ideal that is realized in a very minor way by true particular material statements, and striven for on a grander scale by scientific conceptual schemes. We should indeed be deluded to believe that such schemes do actually realize this ideal, and give us in their field a comprehensive awareness of all there is to know. Science, even the most advanced natural science, is a continuing and developing enterprise filled with probability, though in a few areas approaching the cognitive ideal rather strikingly.

The pragmatist may urge us here to reconsider his case, since we admit that in major instances no final decision between competing conceptual schemes can be reached by purely cognitive means. Why not decide, he may ask, on the basis of which competing scheme is the more serviceable when the whole human situation is taken into account? Plainly, in this loose form pragmatism lets in so many criteria, particularly emotional needs and conational demands, that cognitive decisions would become subject to a wide variety of whim and caprice. Chaos rather than scientific progress would be the outcome. Of course, the cognitive standard can be recast into a pragmatic form using the criterion of cognitive workability. Then, competing conceptual schemes might be said to be true insofar as they worked or brought us to an awareness of the field that truth would, a foretaste infected with generality and probability.

Pragmatism in this tame non-Jamesian form seems acceptable in epistemic inquiry. But it does raise further questions regarding knowledge that require the most careful consideration. I propose to consider most of these questions in the next chapter where the main topic will be the uses and functions of knowledge. But a question repeatedly raised by pragmatic writers might suitably be discussed in this chapter to round out our discussion of the intrinsic features of cognitive content. This question concerns the relation of time and truth: Is truth timeless and eternal, or is it subject to the limitations of time and change?

Eternity

The only reason for holding an assertion about an object to be true is that you are compelled to do so to organize all the relevant detail of your thought into a coherent awareness of the object. When simple material assertions such as "This is a metal" prove themselves in this way, as they endlessly do, we say that they are true or they are truths. Truth is thus a discovery, involved in a temporal process. Yet there are numerous philosophers who say that truth is eternal.

Some eternity philosophers say that truth is fixed forever, and never grows, diminishes, or changes in any way. In their view, there is objectively no new truth, only truth new to this person or that, subjectively new. In consistency these philosophers exclude all particular material statements from truth. Indeed, they exclude the whole realm of becoming and the particular objects of everyday life. Only opinion is possible here. But the fact is that there *are* particular material truths ("This is a metal"), and this seems sufficient and even overwhelming evidence that the view of these eternity philosophers, at least in some respects, must be mistaken.

At the other extreme are those philosophers who model all truth on particular material truths. They also say that any statement, if true at all, is true only for the object in question, and at the time the statement is made. The world is constantly changing, and a true account of the world and of the objects in it must change with it. This view has considerable plausibility, for surely if the world changes, our account of it and of its items must change. However, this does not make truth a mere pawn of time without an extension into eternity. Whether the world changes or not, a particular material statement such as "This is a metal," meaning "The item here in S at this time T is a metal," if true, is always true. Truth is that way. It has an eternity of its own, a circumscribed eternity, and a statement, once true, is true, in the limited way it is true, not merely for the moment but for ever and ever.

Eternity philosophers in the past have confused being and our knowledge of being. These are two, one transhuman and one human, each with its own unique properties and its own type of eternity. Being may be eternal. But truth is not eternal by copying things eternal. Its eternity is not an imitation. Truth is eternal because it is a fulfillment at a given point of an internal human standard. It meets this standard, and once this has been done, there is nothing beyond this possible, so far as truth is concerned. Truth and knowledge have reached their ultimate. Truth and knowledge may be about anything at all, particular or universal, change or permanence, the temporal and the eternal. But once they have pinpointed what an item in its context is, that is what that item in that context is, forever, so far as knowledge goes.

VII

The Functions of Knowledge

Double Function

Knowledge is probably the most momentous possession of human beings. Our greatest constructive and destructive power, epitomized by scientific technology, derives from it. From earliest times civilizations have been a product of what people knew, of all they had found out about themselves and their world. In personal life no less than in social action, knowledge, or lack of it, shapes most of our important decisions. Why then the slogan "Knowledge for Use"? It seems merely an indication of what is the case. In some situations, it is true, some types of knowledge have no use. They serve no purpose. But change the situation and a use appears. Transpose to a theoretical context an idea with no "practical" value, and it may become invaluable as a stimulus of thinking there. At a minimum all knowledge serves the end of knowing and in this sense always has use, and when a person says that a symbolic array is useless, he can only mean either that it is not knowledge or that it is not serving or cannot serve some end that at the time he wants knowledge to serve.

Function or use is indeed a kind of fourth dimension of knowledge. Besides a material, a form, a content, knowl-

101

edge has purposiveness. It executes a role. Some knowledge does seem to exist idly, as if in a cold-storage vault.
Sentences in a dusty encyclopedia, books on a library shelf,
seem of this sort. But such symbolic arrays are called
knowledge because they are believed to be capable of en-
lightening awareness. Function or use is considered as integral to them as material, form, or content.

Generally speaking, knowledge has two major roles or
uses. The first is intrinsic, as a self-rewarding experience,
as a provider of insight and understanding. This is its intrinsic use, serving a goal attained in itself. The second is
extrinsic, as a means to some end beyond knowledge, a
transcognitive end such as modification of the physical environment as in engineering. This is its extrinsic use. Let
us consider each of these more fully.

Intrinsic Use

Knowledge as serving its intrinsic end might be called pure
knowledge. It is knowledge serving understanding, insight,
terminating in itself. In minor form such knowledge may
occur in everyday life, as when a person says, after hearing
another report: "I was merely curious as to what the real
situation was." But it may occur in many other contexts.
Some philosophers hold that this kind of knowledge occurs
at its best in our most advanced physical sciences where
we penetrate to the basic building blocks of the universe.
On the other hand, critics point out the uncertainty element
in our microphysical information, its restriction to probability, statistical averaging, and hypothetical construction.
The quality of its objectivity seems to leave much to be
desired. Moreover, an investigation, such as a physical
science, so overwhelmingly directed to quantitative matters
and resulting regularly in so many purely physical trans-
formations in engineering, can hardly be said to be disinterested in the largest sense. It seems to be a very

advanced specimen of calculative thinking, whose ultimate concern is to deal with things as utensils or utilities, in terms of their advantage to us in the life of action, rather than in terms of the things themselves. Existentialists who make such criticisms[1] sometimes cite, as the highest fulfillment of the purely cognitive aim, the philosophical characterization of being rather than an advanced natural science. Here the knower "brackets out" the instrumental bias, and opens himself to the features of the universe as they occur in a pure disinterested consciousness. And so far as this is actually done, such philosophy is a striking illustration of the intrinsic cognitive aim in action and the use of cognition for pure illumination. But one wonders why this kind of openness cannot be directed as much to the way things work as to the way things are, to causal structure as to the realm of being. Both lie equally open to our investigation. Moreover, any symbolic system claiming to have the wide sweep of a knowledge of being extends in reference far beyond the observational ranges of human awareness. It must contain elements, if not the same elements, that are as hazy, uncertain, or hypothetical as any to be found in physics.

The fact seems to be that concern of the sort required by the intrinsic end of knowledge is not uniquely illustrated by any type of inquiry. It may occur in everyday life, in natural science, in philosophy. Also, the fulfillment of this end may be complete, partial, or of any degree, in any of these or other areas. All depends on the scope of our concern, our antecedent knowledge, and what we obtain in the investigation. In everyday life, a small awareness—that a patch of sky at the moment is blue, that *A* is now telling the truth—may be as perfect a realization of the intrinsic end of knowledge as we shall ever get, if this information is true, and if it is all we wish to use cognition for in the

[1] Cf. Martin Heidegger, *Discourse on Thinking*, trans. J. M. Anderson and E. H. Freund (New York: Harper & Row, 1966).

situation. The fulfillment of the intrinsic end depends on what we cognitively want and what the situation allows, and all that we want may be possible in diverse types of situations.

This listing of everyday cognition, natural science, and philosophy as able to occupy the same level so far as the intrinsic end of knowledge goes, calls for some modification in detail. People generally believe that science occupies the highest rung on the ladder of knowledge. By science they usually mean natural science, notably physics, pointing to the extraordinary feats of physical technology in addition to the purely cognitive accomplishments credited to it. I shall discuss technology when I consider the extrinsic uses of knowledge in a later section of this chapter. But before doing this, I would like to consider science conceived as an embodiment of the intrinsic end of knowledge, and ask what is essential to it and what is inessential, external, and contingent.

Pure Science

If we think of pure science as merely a search for pure knowledge, what we have just said suggests that it might occur in any situation. But where such a search is very brief and limited, and where the result is small, as in a casual conversation, we hesitate to call any pure knowledge emerging there by the name of science. More seems needed. What are some of the required additions?

The first seems to be a deliberate and sustained period of investigation. Pure science, it is thought, requires an extended detachment and abstraction from other interests in pursuit of the purely cognitive goal. This withdrawal from the world into the laboratory and study is easily misunderstood. It does not mean that the personal traits and ambitions of the investigator, the characteristic practical aims of his society, and the whole impetus of his historical situation vanish from his existence and are replaced by a pure eternal vision. These factors remain and exert a force. But they do not constitute the guide and purpose of the investigator during prolonged stretches of his cognitive activity. They lie in the background. Who would deny that the zeal for power, strength, and security in the natural world, and any number of other noncognitive factors, played a part in the growth of the natural sciences in modern times? Clearly they did. But the foremost necessity for this growth to be a development of pure science was sustained episodes of cognitive effort where all other purposes were subordinated to the aim of finding out the nature of nature and of formulating the results precisely. Such sustained inquiry would seem to be the first additional requisite for the existence of pure science. Two other requisites follow closely on its heels. The first is a method fruitful in sustained inquiry. The second is an object-matter of suitable size and character.

What would be a fruitful method in a pure science? Briefly, it would be a method using symbolic structures that were precise, intelligible, and comprehensive. Precision of symbols would be needed for awareness to discover exactly the nature and details of the field. Intelligibility would be necessary so that awareness in as many centers of investigation as possible might function. Comprehensiveness would be required so that awareness in its achieved width could grasp the nature and details of the field in its greatest extent. Method of this sort calls for immediate illustration, and the most obviously apt illustration is the method in the natural sciences. In their primary descriptive phases, in classification and measurement, for example, these sciences use technical terms and mathematical symbols to record what is being described. Monastically exact symbolic expressions are employed. Furthermore, the components of these expressions and their uses are open to all investigators to learn, and explanations and predictions formulated in terms of them therefore are potentially intelligible to all properly prepared investigators. Finally, beside ceaselessly seeking new details and correlating them in low-order generalizations, the natural sciences try to gather their various generalizations, hypotheses, and theories into formal systems from whose axioms and postulates all other discoverable knowledge of the field can be deduced. A comprehensive systematic conception of the area is the ultimate aim. Thus, in its method a natural science may be said to seek to provide awareness, in maximum width, with a precise grasp of its field in its widest range.[2]

Besides method, the other additional requisite of a pure science is an object-matter of suitable size and character. The modern natural sciences again would seem to furnish the obvious illustration. Nature certainly has suitable size. It is a vast inexhaustible field or complex of fields for sustained investigation. Also, nature's character has fitted the method used by the modern natural sciences as hand to glove. "Nature happens to be so constituted that its course can be described by functional equations, and it is because scientists always found nature to be constituted in this way that they came to develop the mathematical language of functionally connected variables."[3] In other words, in nature the modern investigator has found not only an extensive object-matter for sustained attention, but one that has allowed the development of his characteristic mathematical method.

These three requisites of a pure science—sustained detachment, and a method and object-matter of a certain

[2] Cf. C. J. Ducasse, *Science: Its Nature, Method, and Scope,* Third D. W. Prall Memorial Lecture (Piedmont, Calif.: Prall Memorial Foundation, 1947); A. C. Benjamin, "On Defining Science," *Scientific Monthly,* vol. 68, no. 3, March, 1949.
[3] Arthur Pap, "Does Science Have Metaphysical Presuppositions?," *Readings in the Philosophy of Science,* ed. Feigl and Brodbeck, p. 33.

type—may seem tailored to fit the natural sciences and to make them appear to be the ideal of a pure science. Some wisps of knowledge in everyday life may be as certain as anything in any natural science. But no body of knowledge outside the natural sciences seems to exist which illustrates in any high degree the requisites I have described. Although this may be true, it does not follow that there are no other possibilities which might be developed into pure sciences approaching the range and power of the natural sciences. Nor does it mean that the natural sciences are the perfect embodiment of pure science in all respects. Indeed, the natural sciences have certain defects that suggest that they are only very approximate and far from perfect fulfillments of the requisites of a pure science, and that give reason for considering other possibilities in a more favorable light.

First, as I have already stated, even in some of the most advanced natural sciences the best knowledge is limited to probabilities and statistical averages. The quantitative values assigned to individuals are the average values of a crowd of such individuals. Whether they apply with complete exactness to a given individual is only probable. Second, the laws and theories of all the natural sciences are known to be true only of the few verified instances used to project and check them, and even in this respect they may be overcomplex or insufficient. As later investigation sometimes shows, other instances or the same instances reconsidered may not exactly fit these theories and laws, and the theories and laws must undergo modification. Third, the cognitive concern of the natural sciences is primarily with the mechanical routines and aspects of nature. As Pap has indicated, the natural sciences show us the functionally connected quantities of nature, or, more broadly, the causal structure, what depends on what, in the natural world. If nature is more than a system of quantitative entities with a causal structure, the modern natural sciences will never tell us. Finally, the pure cognitive perspective of these sciences is strongly associated culturally with a limited value outlook, which conceives natural processes and entities as invaluable instruments of power, superior to everything else as means to "practical" ends. This external association does not make these sciences less pure within their own territory, but it does encourage them to stay within the limits of this territory, and on the whole the natural sciences have tended to do so. Thus, like the other factors just enumerated, this cultural connection suggests that the modern natural sciences in certain respects are limited as fulfillments of the ideal of a pure science, and that, if there are other possibilities, they should be considered.

Are there other possibilities, less developed at this time, yet capable of considerable development and having independent values of substantial importance? I think there is at least one such possibility, and I would like now to consider it.

A Second Science

The natural sciences deal with entities and processes that are conditions or means to human ends, or potentially so. The proposal I would like to make is that the realm of ends, no less than this realm of conditions or means, be considered a field for pure science. To be sure, one cannot point to any large body of exact knowledge about ends, such as natural science furnishes about conditions or means. But I think there is nothing inherent in the realm of ends to debar it from being a possible field for pure science.

One is greatly encouraged in this belief by the fact that natural science as an activity is itself a pursuit of ends, and therefore part of the realm of ends. Hence, anything we know about it illustrates knowledge of the realm of ends, and the more we know, the more does a pure science of this realm seem possible. Natural science is more than a method and an object-matter. It aims at certain goals, specifically at a certain goal—knowledge of nature that has precision, objectivity, system, universality, and comprehensiveness. Natural science is shaped by this cognitive end, and in each of its investigations you can see ends at work. An experiment is set up to test hypothesis X. This testing is the end, and everything employed in the experiment—materials, apparatus, arrangements, etc.—is selected with this end in view. The end controls the preparations and experimenter's action. Also, fulfillment of the cognitive end is the principle of evaluation, determining whether hypothesis X is to be accepted or rejected. As a vast activity occurring all over the world in many centers of investigation, natural science indeed has come to embody a system of human ends that has caught the imagination of peoples everywhere. Its purposes, procedures, and results seem possible wherever competent human investigation is possible, and constitute a potential realization of a universal cognitive consciousness.

Natural science as knowledge is revered particularly by those who would restrict all science to natural science. In the preceding paragraph, therefore, I have recited a few elementary facts about natural science to remind such believers that natural science itself belongs squarely in the realm of ends, and that their knowledge about it, however authentic, is not natural science, a knowledge of nature, but a knowledge of an end-directed human activity addressed to nature. Indeed, I would like to take natural science as a kind of paradigm of what is to be found in the realm of ends, and using it as our chief example, to ask how the requisites of a pure science listed above would apply to the inhabitants of this area.

First, sustained detachment, or abstraction over an extended period from all nonepistemic concerns interfering in any way with the purely cognitive aim: this certainly seems possible in regard to the domains in the realm of ends. Thus, in regard to natural science, it is certainly possible to study it for what it is, and to reach certain conclusions about it after sustained investigation: that natural science is an end-directed activity, that it can seek pure knowledge, that it uses the method of observation and hypothesis and theory formation, and much more. Some assertions about natural science made by some investigators might be highly controversial. But so are some assertions about phenomena in their field made by some investigators in any science. Enough about natural science seems established and clear to warrant the belief that this activity can be fruitfully and extensively studied simply for what it is, independent of other concerns, and that the sustained detachment that is the first requisite of a pure science is possible in regard to it.

The second requisite of a pure science I have said is a suitable method. That a method having the precision, intelligibility, and systematic comprehensiveness of natural science has been devised to explore the realm of ends cannot of course be claimed. But that a method capable of yielding substantial cognitive results in the area is possible seems equally evident. The realm of ends is distinguishable from the realm of means. Also, its various domains— knowledge, fine art, education, politics, medicine, all the major fields of human activity—have different central ends however much these ends overlap in certain respects. Thus, a differential characterization of the realm as a whole, and of its various domains, seems possible, if they were elevated to objects of a detached, purely cognitive scrutiny. Discovery of terms to make this characterization precise, intelligible, and comprehensive would remain a problem. But the general method of cognitive inquiry, so brilliantly illustrated by natural science, would be available for this purpose. Observation and theory construction, the projection and testing of hypotheses, could have full application. In the value fields, as in the study of nature, we deal with a two-level phenomenon. There is the observable behavior, and the principle inferred to explain it. In a natural science there is the observed fall of an apple, and inference to the law of gravitation. In a value field there is the observed action of an ethical agent, and inference to a purpose— pleasure, power, benevolence, etc.—to explain the value or disvalue of the action. Indeed, in the realm of ends the investigator has an advantage not open to the natural scientist. He is a participant and not merely an observer. He can know the realm from the inside. In some ways, to be sure, this is a disadvantage. An extra effort is needed for detachment. But it also increases intimacy and a closer knowledge of the realm including its gamut of explanatory principles. That the use of the method of observation and inference in each domain would result in generalizations about the goal-directed activities in these domains, and that these generalizations might ultimately lead investigators to arrange them in some systematic deductive order, seem logical steps in a sustained cognitive articulation of the field. In short, the general features of fruitful method in pure science could characterize the sustained investigation of human ends. The precision, intelligibility, and systematic completeness might not be exactly of the same kind and degree as in physics. But they would be the result of an equally valid method and would be realized more and more fully as the object-matter permitted.

As to this object-matter, its suitability is the third requisite of a pure science. In a value science, this object-matter should not be conceived too narrowly. The primary topic should be the aim structure of the activity since this shapes the activity and its outcome, and includes all of the distinctive value possibilities of the field. But to describe

this aim structure in an illuminating way requires considerable attention to whatever is necessary and useful to
realize it. Ends can be effected only by means working
effectively, and a proper characterization of these means
should therefore be included in a realistic depiction of
ends.

That the object-matter of a value science so understood has the breadth to make it suitable for sustained and
methodical investigation is evident at a glance. Not merely
natural science, but fine art, for example, is a very broad
domain, and with its various subdomains—painting, sculp-
ture, music, and the others—stretches before us a complex
differentiated field of activity with an aim structure and
diversified causal resources. So do education, politics, medicine, and the other human fields. No human domain com-
pares in sheer spatial extent with nature, the object-matter
of natural science. But in inner complexity, subtlety, and
variety of purpose, the larger human domains are equally
challenging and obviously extensive fields for inquiry. Nor
do the means or causal resources at their disposal raise
puny problems for analysis and description. Each field here
presents challenges to cognition of considerable magnitude,
and from the technical standpoint, if from no other, challenges worthy of the most methodical scientific scrutiny.

On the basis of the foregoing remarks about object-
matter, method, and detachment, I think we can say not
that a second pure science exists, but that it is possible.
Much remains to be done: concerted technical effort, bring-
ing about favorable social circumstances. But the possibility
of a second pure science parallel to pure natural science
seems clear enough, I think, from the above inspection of
its territory and nature.[4]

[4] Gotshalk, *Patterns of Good and Evil,* chap. 7, and *idem, Human
Aims in Modern Perspective* (Yellow Springs, Ohio: Antioch Press),
chaps. 5 and 6, discuss and illustrate in much more detail this proposal of a value science.

Reductionism

In their zeal to be considered scientific, some philosophers have advocated the extension of natural science into the human domains and the reduction of inquiry there to a branch of natural inquiry. Up to a certain point this extension is not only legitimate but necessary. The human being is a part of nature. His behavior employs physical and other natural processes and techniques to effect its ends. Delineation of how these work, the causal structures involved, is a needed part of our knowledge of the human domains. This is true not merely of individuals but also of institutions and societies. To depict how exactly they work —their machinery and its operations—is to contribute to our understanding of the human scene. A social science, as Boulding has said, would contain "a sound knowledge of the structure and dimensions of society, and of the causal relations which are at work determining the movement of its innumerable interrelated variables."[5] This would be to make social science into natural science and place human society in the general natural science orbit.

A long line of modern thinkers, from Hobbes to John Watson and beyond, go much further than this. They hold that the mechanical concept contains the only truth about human behavior, and is certainly the only basis for scientific knowledge in the human area. Our view, which is directly opposed to this, is that the human domains open up unique branches of pure research additional to natural science research, and that these domains are not reducible to merely causal domains. Something important has been omitted when you conceive them in this way.

The main argument against reductionism can be stated several ways, but perhaps the simplest is a recital of elementary fact. Among the most solid components of our

[5] Kenneth E. Boulding, *The Organizational Revolution* (New York: Harper & Bros., 1953), pp. xiii-xiv.

human knowledge is our awareness of ourselves as purposive beings. We seek ends and constantly strive for goals, and we know we do, and we know the reductionist does, especially when he tries to triumph over us with his arguments. Moreover, seeking ends, striving for goals, is not just one thing causing another. It is also, uniquely, setting up standards, erecting measuring rods, implying what must happen for value to be obtained. Were this end-side of our being cut out and our actions reduced to purely causal sequences, events would occur, but all criteria for measuring their value, particularly the worth of things for the striving agent, would be gone, and human life would be reduced to value vacuous motion. The reductionist position, as hinted above, has also its budget of paradoxes. The self-determinacy on which natural science rests, the ability of the scientist to choose his field and to direct his inquiry by his own ends is founded on his purposiveness. Without purposiveness, this ability to choose and direct would vanish. Thus reductionism, aiming to promote the supremacy of natural science, would destroy the very condition of the natural science process.[6]

Although our concept of a second science implies the rejection of reductive naturalism, it does not at all imply the rejection of natural science. This remains a body of knowledge of high stature, and, extended into the human domain, is invaluable in several respects, chiefly two. First, it illumines a major side or aspect of human activity, the mechanical aspect, or how human individuals and institutions operate, independent of whether this operation is good or bad. Second, as I have already indicated, its cognitive procedures of gathering data, putting forth theories, seeking verification, organizing its lower-level generalizations under conceptual schemes, suggest parallels for value

[6] Cf. David Bidney, *Ideological Differences and World Order,* ed. F. S. C. Northrop (New Haven: Yale University Press, 1963), p. 350.

science, not models to be slavishly followed, but models with adaptable features, recommended by their fruitfulness.

Technology

The human being is capable of a triple awareness. He can be aware of his environment, aware of himself with his purpose structure, and aware of these other two types of awareness. Natural science has its basic orientation in the first type of awareness; value science in the second; while philosophy rests on the most comprehensive awareness of all. The intrinsic value achieved by these forms of awareness might be described as insight, disclosure of the precise character of what is there. In natural science, the insight is into the vast outlay of nature. In value science, the insight is into human motives and goals. But all such knowledge (also philosophical knowledge) can have uses beyond insight. All can be used to produce results in transcognitive areas. These results may range from a wonderful new drug or medicine to a devastating new weapon system, from liberating and tranquilizing an anxiety-ridden psyche to motivational deceptions in advertising and politics. Perhaps the most comprehensive and spectacular example of this transcognitive use of knowledge is technology understood in the usual sense. A brief discussion of it will amply illustrate what is meant by the extrinsic as contrasted with the intrinsic use of knowledge.

In its usual sense, modern technology is natural knowledge applied to physical materials to produce utilities— bridges, roads, automobiles, electric circuits, etc. It is a flower of natural knowledge become belief in Bain's sense, that upon which a man is prepared to act.[7] The products of this technology are so numerous and familiar in daily life that we assume we understand perfectly the process

[7] Alexander Bain, *The Emotions and the Will* (New York: D. Appleton and Company, 1888).

behind them. Yet there is a depth to our technology that does not meet the eye. The causal laws of heat and electricity may be discovered by investigation, yet remain sterile technologically. What is needed is a Watt or Edison who can translate general principles into particular embodiments. This translation takes an altogether different type of talent from talent in pure scientific research, namely, a talent for imaginative design.[8] Between pure theory and a useful invention is a great gap, and a resourceful imagination must mediate between them. This imaginative process has its cognitive features, but in this context it has not primarily a cognitive aim. Its aim is to provide an instrument of transcognitive action, except, of course, where its aim is to design better apparatus for conducting research into nature.

Need technology be confined to the production of physical instruments? Given suitable imagination, I think it might flourish in any field where sufficient basic knowledge exists. In particular, I think it might flourish in the realm of ends if sufficient pure knowledge of the scientific type were developed there. Indeed, it does already exist there in some areas. In medicine, for instance, there is not only considerable causal knowledge, knowledge of physics, chemistry, physiology, etc., but health as an aim or end, and the requisites for realizing this end, are being slowly understood. As a result, procedures have been designed over the years to realize this end and meet these requisites, and these guide lines, which are really normative patterns for achieving health, are taught in medical colleges. Such procedures for effecting a particular normative result in action constitute a technology in the value area. To be sure, this technology is not the invention of physical instruments —these might result—but of patterns of action, chiefly patterns of remedial action. The main point, however, is that

[8] Whitehead, *Science and the Modern World*, p. 141.

it is the production of a transcognitive result in a value domain on the basis of a knowledge of means and ends, which for some time have been given considerable scientific attention.

In any human domain whose end is known and the requisites for realizing this end are understood, this kind of normative technology is theoretically possible. Let me illustrate this with an audacious example. If it were possible to develop in the scientific manner described in the two preceding sections a theory of a good society, and if a wide and deep knowledge of the means available to realize such a society were at hand, capable imagination steeped in the social actualities could produce effective normative projections. A theory of a good society as precisely developed as the theory of heat in physics could be as sound a basis for the invention of laws and social rules as the theory of heat for the production of steam engines. As it was in medicine, the first problem would be to obtain authentic pure knowledge of the field, here an adequate concept of social means and ends. With such knowledge, practical imagination would still be needed. But with a concept of social order of the broad cognitive quality of a physical theory, imaginative leadership could produce social constructions, even social marvels, comparable to the machines we owe to the technology based on physics. It would of course be a technology of norms rather than of things. The products would be particular patterns of public behavior rather than physical instruments enhancing the causal power of human beings.[9]

In the next chapter, I shall discuss why this elementary and important project is still only a dreamy possibility, and more generally, why adequate normative investigation, ex-

[9] Gotshalk, in *Human Aims in Modern Perspective,* Chap. 5, "The Political Situation," and chap. 6, "New Politics," discusses this possibility in more detail.

cept in medicine, is in such a backward condition. But to continue the present discussion: in any inquiry about a society, two aspects should be distinguished. One aspect is concerned with what things have happened and/or how they happened: the statistics of births and deaths in a city, a nation, the planet; the variations in rural communities of the rate of marriage with the rate of crop production; fuel consumption and temperature variations in a geographic area; the ups and downs of the business cycle, and much more. Inquiry of this sort is an application of the natural science outlook to the social realm, seeking a description of the mechanisms at work or of the results of their workings. But besides an interest in the causal processes of society, a social inquirer may be interested in its unresolved problems. The problems of war, unemployment, overpopulation, poverty, political instability, the clash of races and cultures—these indicate a few of the widespread imperfections in society in our day. These problems are not solved by describing how they happened. They require a concept of social good in terms of which social eyesores are eyesores. Equally they require procedures based on such a concept to guide action into paths that would remove or avoid these eyesores. This type or aspect of social inquiry is what value science and its technology would be concerned with.[10]

It may be objected that such a technology would tend to robotize people, to straitjacket them into uniform patterns and drain from them all their color, individuality, and humanity. I do not think so. Of course, given ill will, knowledge of the purest sort can be used to repress and shackle people. But I am discussing knowledge being used to generate a genuinely good society, and imaginative projections

[10]Cf. F. A. Hayek, *Individualism and Economic Order* (Chicago: University of Chicago Press, 1948), p. 57, where a distinction is drawn between two aspects of social inquiry similar to the one in this paragraph.

with the same intent. Such projections would always have to prove themselves in concrete existence just as a bridge, a road, or an automobile must. They would have to be good in practice. And if they did not amplify our humanity and lead to the good, they would be rejected, as false hypotheses are. They would have failed to fulfill the intent for using them.

The knowledge we live by today extends far beyond natural science, its technology, and the know-how that enables us to use and repair the physical instruments produced by this technology. This knowledge includes a vast wealth of factual detail—that eggs break, that Stalin is dead, ad infinitum. It also includes some knowledge of the purposes of other people and of the goals we ourselves believe to be worthwhile. This knowledge of purposes is defective, but not merely in the sense that we are unclear or ignorant about many purposes we or others pursue. It is defective in the sense that many ends knowingly pursued are the source of destructive consequences. They maim human values. That our ends therefore should be given the most sustained scrutiny, and that some better conception of what people can profitably seek together is desirable, seems evident enough, and considering the centrality of purpose in the human being, a great urgency, as well as considerable importance, obviously should attach to such a sustained study. But the modern emphasis has been all the other way. It has been toward a consummate knowledge of natural processes rather than a scientific knowledge of human goals. How can this emphasis be explained? What are its current consequences? What are the prospects for altering it? Can the structure of awareness include any other emphasis that is relevant and promising?

VIII

The Modern Situation

Social Context

The intellectual life, I have said, is a knowledge-seeking and a knowledge-enjoying life, or that part of our life devoted primarily to the consideration of situations challenging our cognitive powers. How much of our life is intellectual depends on numerous factors, but mainly two: personal inclination and social context. In extreme circumstances, as when one is under bombardment during a war, purely intellectual activity may completely disappear. Under certain inner conditions—intense anxiety or boredom—the requisite personal inclination may be lacking. But the chief personal and social factors on which the intellectual life depends are not such intermittent and fluctuating conditions. They are the main bent of a person's nature and the dominant value-bent of his society.

To be devoted unreservedly to the intellectual life requires a certain kind of mentality, a Cartesian type, detached, critical, contemplative, creative. Such minds spring up in all ages. They exist today as in the seventeenth century. It is a mind that delights conspicuously in free speculation, in creative discovery, in circumspect intelligence. It is a rare human phenomenon, and combined with

120

genius of extraordinary power, it may exemplify a supreme quality of an age, as Descartes did. Such a mentality has certain obvious components. Temperament or inborn intellectual inclination is one, native agility another. So is an "instinct" to avoid in appreciable degree what usually would interfere with its development. But where such mentality comes to exemplify current intellectual power, a sizable opportunity for its exercise also exists in its day. The milieu or social context indeed might be described as the crowning condition of intellectual eminence. It is called upon to supply a whole galaxy of favorable circumstances. These begin with the economic. A Descartes without an inheritance or similar provision would have encountered serious difficulties. A starving or economically rundown community is not likely to give strong support to purely intellectual endeavor. But the requisite social conditions for intellectual eminence are more than economic. What are some of them?

One is a number of persons, not just a few geniuses, active in intellectual pursuits and concerned with a diversity of problems in various related areas. Intellectual creativity thrives where swarms of talent are at work, and the great ages of intellectual advance are the results not merely of the giants but also of the stimulating work of many diverse but so-called minor talents.

A second favorable social condition is some system of communication between these intellectuals. To develop clear and coherent concepts ordinarily requires withdrawal from so-called life demands and a certain isolation. To be out of communication with others including other intellectuals is often the beginning of wisdom. But a prolonged isolation has obvious hazards. One may rework ground already well-worked. One may lose the challenge that the contrary or parallel insights of others make. In communication with others, stepping stones sought for in vain in isolation may be found without delay, and directions that had seemed quixotic or utopian may prove clearly acceptable. To be sure, a communication system including letters, periodicals, and books freely circulated, visits, consultations, and meetings, may become clogged with such an abundance of material as to seem a nuisance. But selection and simplification according to need can usually overcome this defect for the creative intellect whose mind has suitable focus.

A third favorable social condition of intellectual eminence is some active cooperation among intellectual workers. By this is meant: an interest in reaching a common understanding of problems and fields, and in methods suitable for dealing with these problems and fields; the using of the results of one set of investigations as the basis of another set of investigations; the division or significant nonduplication of undertakings, and the like. Such cooperation can greatly quicken advances in technique and knowledge as well as stimulate a friendly social feeling conducive to intensified competitive effort.

Supplementing this third condition, a fourth would be a system of education introducing the unadvanced mind to the elements and background of current intellectual activities, and challenging the advanced mind to bring together more coherently the great variety of new understanding flowing from this activity. In this education every effort would be made to include as many as qualify. The gifted and temperamentally suited are not innumerable, and may exist in any stratum of society. Educational opportunity would therefore be conscientiously extended throughout the total society.

It may be objected that these four conditions—education, cooperation, communication, numerous intellectual workers, and also talent, inclination, and economic support —have existed in appreciable degree for some time in the Western world. Yet it cannot be said that now, or during the last hundred years, we have lived in a society dominated by the intellectual life, nor that the intellectual has been the master and shaper of our history. Much more central throughout the whole modern period have been other figures—military, political, commercial, financial, industrial. These people have been the masters of the modern world, the shapers of its history, and only because they have used the fruits of certain intellectual pursuits, notably the technologies based on modern science, has the intellectual life been projected toward the center of the modern stage and attained such social centrality and prosperity as it has had.

This objection is well taken, and calls for some amplification of what I have just said. The social conditions I have listed, or some of them, and the factors of talent, inclination, and economic support, should be described as necessary for high-grade intellectual activity in a society. But they are not sufficient to make intellectual activity a dominant department there, or to make it dominant in shaping a society's decisive historical events. Something more is needed, something which extends beyond the inhabitants and intramural conditions of the domain of knowledge. This is a fundamental value inclination permeating the whole social order. Such an inclination generates the hierarchy of domains to be found in any society.

Post-Medieval Bent

What has been the chief value inclination in modern society insofar as it has influenced the intellectual life? If we can trust the early modern philosophers as spokesmen for post-medieval intentions, the initial value bent of the modern world was toward glorification of the natural human being, developing fully his propensities, the building of a paradise in the natural world, the construction of a kingdom of man. This was the ideology of the Renaissance expressed by certain Italian thinkers, and by Erasmus, Rabelais, and Francis Bacon. Humanism with earthly overtones was the inspiration. Under this aegis, clearly the intellectual life should have surged forward, and indeed it did. But other intentions were also at hand, and gave events a curious and more characteristic direction.

One great break with the medieval past, ultimately realigning intellectually all Western endeavor, was the Copernican revolution, which set forth a new mathematical conception of the physical world. This revolution, as advanced by Kepler, Galileo, and others, lighted the sky with a new revelation, arousing the inquisitive talents of Europe to reexamine all the workings of physical nature. This was indeed badly needed. The conventional medieval investigator had added little to the ancient Greek knowledge of the physical world except teleological embroidery. The time was more than ripe to strip physical nature to her working parts, and to learn how it was made and what could be expected from it. And this was not only needed; it was opportune. It fitted into the new humanism, or seemed to. If the human being planned to develop the natural world into a kingdom of man, it would be fitting and important to know how it was made, and how to control it. The upshot was not only a new mathematical science of nature following the quantitative aspects of the Copernican model, but the prospect of a technology capable of shaping and controlling physical processes with great exactness.

It is not possible to fault this development seriously when taken in isolation. It meant a lively intellectual life for an ever-expanding number of investigators. It meant a considerable increase in the causal control of the environment that could be used to enhance the health, range, efficiency, and opportunity of man in nature. And today it still comprises an asset of incalculable value. But viewed from a larger, society-wide perspective this development had from the beginning important shortcomings. They are typified by Descartes. Any reader of the *Discourse on Method* cannot but be impressed by the modest claims the author makes for his method, and the quiet boldness of his major projects. Yet throughout the *Discourse* there is a certain pretense and deviousness that makes one suspect that things are not always being presented exactly as they are. In Part III the reader comes upon a set of rules of conduct that the author has decided to follow in his public actions while he pursues his intellectual method in private. At first glance, these rules seem no more than various ways of abstracting from practical concerns so as to allow full attention to intellectual endeavor—very proper cautions. But more closely examined they amount to a resolve by the intellectual to take no real part at all in practical affairs or in the direction of society. Our author will acquiesce in the status quo, and should misfortune strike him, he will attempt to reform himself rather than social conditions. The conduct and guidance of the public and institutional world he will turn over to others already active who are more experienced and competent than he is to perform such tasks.

Were this resolve of Descartes's purely personal, it would be interesting only autobiographically. But it typifies so much more. It is an early modern declaration of what is known today as value-free science or science proclaiming ethical neutrality, and typifies an attitude to which an increasingly large segment of modern scientists gradually turned with considerable vehemence. According to this attitude, the world of human conduct and practical affairs, with its clashes of preferences, its value conflicts and strivings, is completely outside the purview of science.

It is difficult to determine all that was behind this modern turn of events, but some of the factors must have been these: the great success of the new physical sciences as intellectual endeavors and their great intellectual fruitfulness; the zest outside science for enlarged physical power to which the new sciences with their dedication to the causal understanding and control of nature promised to contribute abundantly; the strong, even absolute, claim of entrenched power centers, religious and political chiefly, rightfully to guide and rule the conduct of men, declaring these practical areas still sacred ground, as intellectual sovereignty over the physical area slipped increasingly from their grasp; finally, the continued response of the physical realm to the expanding techniques of the new research, so that this realm seemed, as it still seems, an endlessly fascinating and easily sufficient field in which to exert all the intellectual ingenuity that the human being can summon.

But however one explains the turn modern science took, the fact is that it did take this turn. Moreover, it flourished. Natural science extended its reach from exact investigations of the physical world to almost equally extensive investigations of living and human beings. To Copernicus and Newton and Einstein were added the names of Darwin and Mendel and Freud. But because science in this form won out, it had devastating, as well as fruitful, consequences.

Consequences

In describing the consequences of modern science, it has been customary in the past to dwell on its astonishing achievements. These have been impressive, particularly the large and ever-growing body of exact knowledge, and the powerful technology based on this knowledge and resulting in novel transportation systems, world-spanning communication systems, mass production methods in agriculture and industry, and so much more. But lately the praise has turned to dispraise. Eulogy has given way to anxiety and dread. The antihuman effects of our scientific technology on the teeming life that has enjoyed its fruits have become the focus of general attention. It is almost as if a monster of incalculable destructive powers had suddenly been discovered in our midst.

The dehumanizing consequences of our technology on modern living could have been discerned in miniature over a hundred years ago in the small industrial towns of England where the Industrial Revolution flowing from modern science began. Here the production of goods was enlarged and accelerated by new methods. But the human side of life, the unhealthy and cheerless working and living conditions, already foreshadowed what was to emerge on a much larger scale in the latter part of the twentieth century. Today it is as if the tiny virus in the old industrial towns was spreading rapidly toward a world-wide infection. As our modern technological powers have been increased and diversified, they have been employed in at least three very harmful ways. First, their facilities and products have poured and continue to pour ever larger quantities of dangerous pollutants into the rivers, lakes, seas, soil, and atmosphere, and have harmed incalculably the earth's vegetation and animal life. Second, the prosperity of our technological power has encouraged populations to grow enormously in Western nations. Living space has shrunk alarmingly. The commodious life for all has become more and more a fantasy, and the world food supply—already insufficient—promises to become increasingly insufficient, as modern techniques exhaust the not infinite resources of the planet. Finally, our technological power has produced weapon systems capable of destroying quickly the entire human race and probably all of life as we know it. These consequences of our scientific technology present the human race today with three prospects, all grim. The first is to suffocate in its own effluvia. The second is mass and possibly general starvation. The third is a nuclear holocaust. At the present rapidly accelerating rate of social change, any one of these possibilities or any combination might easily be realized by the end of the century, or shortly thereafter.

How did all of this come about? Why do we face such grim prospects? I have said that it is the result of employing modern scientific technology, and so it is. But the more accurate explanation is really different. The flaw is not in science and technology but in the ends we have pursued and in the way we have pursued them. It was not Galileo, but the political, military, commercial, and other modern men with their surpassing practical sagacity who started us down this inclined plane and whose goals continue to accelerate our descent.

To contrast with the medieval, the modern world professed a supreme concern for the natural man. To build him an earthly paradise, a humanist kingdom in a natural setting—this was its alleged objective. But the practical men of the modern world, not the philosophers, had other ideas. As the technologies of modern science produced their marvelous methods of harnessing nature, these political, military, industrial, commercial, financial, and other leaders inserted their own ends into these processes. Their goals were numerous, but chiefly these: power, wealth, status, efficiency, control. More generally, the goals were self-aggrandizement—individual, corporative, national. The key consideration was not what humane uses could be made of these novel processes, but how much self-power they could be turned into. This divisive and destructive self-centered hedonism is still the dominant motive of human action in our times, and it is this derangement in the realm of ends, not the magnificent technical advances made in the realm of means, that primarily accounts for the grim prospects of the human race at the present.[1]

[1] Cf. D. W. Gotshalk, *The Promise of Modern Life* (Yellow Springs, Ohio: Antioch Press, 1958), chap. 4.

Had this been otherwise—had the early modern concept of a kingdom of man been a serious practical idea, not a philosophical slogan, had the necessarily long and painful attention been given to it such as natural science gave to working out its new idea of the physical world, had the development of our means and the harnessing of nature been strictly controlled by this idea—the more violent and spectacular tragedies of modern history, so colorful to describe, so debilitating to endure, would certainly have been avoided, and something like the life early modern thinkers envisioned would have been possible. This long-ago opportunity is now only a dream painful to recall. In place of it, modern practical men started a runaway process of disemboweling nature to enhance their sovereignty, while the ordinary mortal in bedazzled innocence began to sleepwalk toward his own destruction.

I think there is little doubt about what is fundamentally needed. In broadest terms, it is to put in control of the human family a concept of its well-being that is theoretically well established, and to redirect all use of our vast natural and technological resources to fulfilling in practice the requirements of this concept. The first great problem is to develop such a concept. It took natural scientists from Copernicus to Newton to establish a fully adequate theoretical foundation. Perhaps this time can be shortened. The second great problem is to get such a concept placed in control of human affairs, an even greater problem. Clearly, at this late date, neither of these problems can be solved very quickly. That would require a sudden and very radical awakening all over the earth, which seems most unlikely. But something can be done, a start made. In any case, only in the degree that these problems are solved and some theoretical and practical rectification is made in the realm of ends can the prospects of the human being be brightened.

Rectification

This rectification brings us back to the second science of which I have already written. Several points about this second science should be given special emphasis in the present connection.

First, the primary aim of the second science, even conjoined with the purpose of practical rectification, would be cognitive, not practical. This aim would be to uncover what the human being is as a creature of ends, what broadly he needs for health and general well-being on this planet, what specific ends have proved themselves, or promise to prove themselves, as fit embodiments of these broader needs, and what means tapped in what way would strengthen rather than cripple or fail to promote the fulfillment of these needs. All such inquiry would have strong practical implications, and, as it succeeded, it would probably lead almost imperceptibly into a social technology designed to put its findings into practice. But the inquiry itself would be an effort to become aware of how certain matters stand. It would be guided by this cognitive aim, and in this sense it would be a theoretical and intellectual inquiry, and not a form of practical action.

Second, it should be realized that whether this type of inquiry is instituted or not, human beings will be governed by ends, and values will play a decisive role in their lives. Modern natural science, as I have mentioned, is sometimes said to be value-free, reporting coldly and objectively the stubborn hard facts of nature independent of any value perspective. But modern natural science is really a value activity. It is a purposive pursuit with its own standards and ends, and it sifts everything through this system of ends. You do not escape values by being "scientific." Indeed, "scientific" is a value, a kind of eminence we place on a certain grade of knowledge, and on certain methods and attitudes. No human activity, except possibly the briefest mechanical action, eludes the realm of ends and the scrutiny of standards. The question that the proposed rectification raises is not whether science shall become entangled for the first time in the realm of value, but whether human beings want to continue to pursue crudely understood ends, distorting their lives, or whether they want to discover the best ends possible, and the best means to their realization.

The desirability of an enlarged understanding of what we should do, if it can be achieved, seems obvious enough. But it has its subtleties also. When the good is known less well than things, says Socrates, then the value even of things is missed. This is our condition: a superior knowledge of things, a confused ascientific knowledge of the good. The elevation of the latter to the cognitive status of the former would mean a surer and clearer understanding not only of the ends to be sought, but also of the best direction in which to apply our means. It would thus enhance the value of things, so far as human benefit was concerned.

The great problem remains: Can the proposed rectification be achieved in any effective degree? Can the modern emphasis up to now in the domain of knowledge and technology be enlarged so as to include equally the second science and its technology? The problem is partly technical: Does the human being have the intellectual capacity to explore the realm of ends and come up with insights that can be developed into a genuine science and scientific technology? But in addition to this technical problem there is a complex practical problem: Can these technical results be achieved in time, and if so, will human beings generally accept them and put them into effect? A decisive answer to this second question especially, but really to both, cannot be given at the present time. Optimists will have their opinions. Pessimists will have theirs. But actually the answer rests upon things still uncertain, such as the effect on human beings of the emerging social climate and the emerging course of social events.

The domain of knowledge, I have said, has always been affected by the character of the social climate. A strong current of anti-intellectualism shapes it one way. In America particularly anti-intellectualism has had considerable vigor. Evangelical religion with its unreconstructed fundamentalism, egalitarian democracy with its strong leveling tendencies, business enterprise with its emphasis on action and profits, pragmatic education with its accent on life-adjustment, have captivated large segments of the populace,[2] and deprecated the intellectual as a strange untrustworthy creature. Generally, the modern masses have accepted the technological fruits of the intellectual's work, but, unless his work has had such fruits, they have been suspicious of him and his ideas. As a consequence, the modern intellectual often has felt that he had only two choices—to be a tool or an outsider, a "hireling or hermit."[3] And where he has not hired himself out, he has tended to retire into himself. "Thus, in the modern world, the celibacy of the medieval learned class has been replaced by a celibacy of the intellect which is divorced from the concrete contemplation of the complete facts. . . . In short, the specialized functions of the community are performed better and more progressively, but the generalized direction lacks vision. The progressiveness in detail only adds to the danger produced by the feebleness of coordination."[4]

However, social climates change, and in recent times, so far as the domain of knowledge is concerned, many changes have seemed for the better. "Egghead" is still a

[2] Cf. Richard Hofstadter, *Anti-Intellectualism in American Life* (New York: Alfred A. Knopf, 1963).
[3] Eric Bentley, *A Century of Hero Worship* (Philadelphia: J. B. Lippincott Co., 1944), p. 287.
[4] Whitehead, *Science and the Modern World,* p. 283.

term of disparagement. But mingled with this attitude is often a certain fear and envy, and even a faint admiration. During very recent decades, the role of the highly educated person in public life, particularly in industry and politics, has increased enormously. The obviously great dependence of our civilization on scientific and technical knowledge has brought about a great change in popular attitudes toward learning and education. Combined with continued high-grade performance, it has given the accomplishments of the intellectual a new and elevated status. Knowledge itself has become a big business. Not merely publishers, governments, manufacturers, and other special interests, but people generally want to share in its dividends. This popular enthusiasm by itself certainly will not generate the rectifying changes we have described as necessary. But it does indicate that the intellectual life is much closer to general social acceptance, and this is highly favorable to initiative that would attempt to effect the required rectifications.

Permanent Virtues

In any human domain almost anything can be accomplished by talent and a united social will, if the final hour has not passed. But we should always remember that the domain of knowledge is not dependent for its strength merely on social contingencies. Whatever the external weather, it has its own distinctive internal excellences, negative and positive, and in conclusion I would like to describe very briefly one or two of these.

Long ago, Plato noticed that a person deeply devoted to the pursuit of knowledge, like Socrates, had turned his back on hatred, malice, greed, and the other disturbing impulses which animate the spiritually rootless. Later, Spinoza demonstrated that in the presence of active intellectual endeavor the life of passion sinks below the threshold of interest and attention. It may recur in the individual afterward, even in accentuated form. But it is much more likely to recur moderated by the enlightened devotion to intellectual pursuits, as bad habits are weakened by good.

But more important than these negative virtues are certain positive excellences. Chief here is the centrality of intellectual effort in answering our inescapable questions. The human being, as the saying goes, is born into a world he did not make. But he is obliged to find out what he can make of it. His many needs require that he make something of it. But what? To find answers to this question or set of questions is the prime responsibility of man's intellectual power, and to provide insight and enlightenment here in ever greater abundance is one of the prime glories of the intellectual life. There are numerous substitutes for this intellectual effort—magic, witchcraft, superstition, etc. But they give only ersatz satisfaction, not the certainties and demonstrable probabilities that successful intellectual inquiry provides. This intellectual excellence has become distributed over many areas. The symbolic logician who spins out fine webs of abstract order may seem to be idling over trivial puzzles. Yet his production may yield unforeseen novelties, from a new insight into formal order to a new way of looking at mathematics or programming a computer. But however this power of the intellect is distributed, it comes to much the same thing. Its virtue is to provide, as abundantly as the human being can, the answers—few as they are—that *do* answer his problems, and not to put him off with substitutes that block his path to discovering the certainties and demonstrable probabilities that he can.

This excellence of the intellectual life is not an easy virtue. Indeed, only because the mind is invaded with perplexity, discontent, and uncertainty does this virtue exist vigorously, or at all. Perhaps this is a saving grace. The required turmoil gives the intellectual life a dynamism that all fruitful activity needs. But it also creates tensions, painful suspense, and obstacles, and it lowers expectations, acutely so for those who can abide only solutions. Nevertheless, the attractiveness of the intellectual life remains very strong to the intellectually inclined. Of natural science Bronowski writes: "Ours is a vision and an activity . . . science is a complete culture."[5] In a sense, of course, science, even in its broadest meaning, is not a complete culture. A social setting with useful pragmatic arrangements, among congenial people, seems as necessary to a complete culture. But there is something completely satisfying in the intellectual life at its most excellent.

As I have tried to indicate, the intellectual life, as well as its central virtue, has tremendous range. In most playful form, it occurs in bantering conversation where wisecracks, puns, and gags are used for fun to characterize people or topical events in their picturesque immediacy, and it reaches out from this into all sorts of contexts, some practical and others as withdrawn as scholarly cloisters. In our effort to give some prominence in our discussions to the natural and value sciences, we have put no emphasis at all on what some regard as the highest form of the intellectual life. This supreme form is what philosophers from Plato and Aristotle onward called first philosophy. In Plato's phrase, first philosophy is a concern for all time and existence, and modern philosophers from Descartes and Spinoza to Bergson and Whitehead, no less than the ancients, have seen in it the opportunity to exercise the cognitive powers as far as they can reach. This most complete form of intellectual activity would seem to require that if it were loved at all it would be loved for its own sake. But devotion to it is not without its instrumental values. Indeed, Socrates recommended it as a crowning reward for his philosopher

[5] Bronowski, "The Abacus and the Rose," p. 17.

kings, an agreeable vacation from the narrower problems and confusions of mortal existence that had been confronting them. However, it was its inner excellence, its luminous contact with the hem of all existence in eternity, that gave this most complete form of the intellectual life its stature among the giants of speculation. It defined for them the apex of the structure of awareness.

Index of Proper Names

A Note on the Author

D. W. Gotshalk is professor of philosophy, emeritus, at the University of Illinois. Born in Trenton, New Jersey, he received his A.B. from Princeton University and his Ph.D. from Cornell University. In his distinguished career he has served as chairman of the University of Illinois Department of Philosophy, president of the Western Division of the American Philosophical Association, chairman of the APA National Board of Officers, president of the American Society for Aesthetics, and fellow of the American Association for the Advancement of Science. His other books are: *Structure and Reality* (1937, 1968), *Metaphysics in Modern Times* (1940), *Art and the Social Order* (1947, 1963), *The Promise of Modern Life* (1958), *Patterns of Good and Evil* (1963), and *Human Aims in Modern Perspectives* (1966).

UNIVERSITY OF ILLINOIS PRESS